Down-to-Earth Angels

Down-to-Earth Angels

Letters from the Heavens

Donna Allen

iUniverse, Inc.
New York Lincoln Shanghai

Down-to-Earth Angels
Letters from the Heavens

Copyright © 2005 by Donna Allen

All rights reserved. No part of this book may be used or reproduced by any means, graphic, electronic, or mechanical, including photocopying, recording, taping or by any information storage retrieval system without the written permission of the publisher except in the case of brief quotations embodied in critical articles and reviews.

iUniverse books may be ordered through booksellers or by contacting:

iUniverse
2021 Pine Lake Road, Suite 100
Lincoln, NE 68512
www.iuniverse.com
1-800-Authors (1-800-288-4677)

ISBN-13: 978-0-595-35575-4 (pbk)
ISBN-13: 978-0-595-80059-9 (ebk)
ISBN-10: 0-595-35575-7 (pbk)
ISBN-10: 0-595-80059-9 (ebk)

Printed in the United States of America

To Our Grandsons,

Tyler James and Aiden Benjamin,
who live on this side of the veil
And Our Granddaughter,
Leah Rose,
who lives on the other

CONTENTS

Introduction 1

Listing of Recipients and Angels 5

Chapter One   Across the Veil 9

Chapter Two   Angel Letters 29

Chapter Three   A Session with Neal: Be Your Joy 235

Closing Thoughts 245

Acknowledgments

I give thanks to:

Richard Allen, my husband, for his continual love and support

Louise Cook, an angel intuitive, for introducing me to my angel, Marc

Dorie Cerny, for her friendship and support and for offering suggestions to the original manuscript

Mary Ellen Lucas, for sharing her spiritual gifts and for her gentleness and sensitivity

Neal Szpatura, for being my teacher and friend and always nudging me forward

Ginny Botz, my dear sister and lifelong spiritual confidante

Greg Cosimi, for sharing his computer expertise

Ellie Vayo, for photographing me as well as my drum

Tina Fisher, for her intuitive insights, for drawing the graphics, and for painting my drum, which is depicted on the cover of the book

Henry Reed and Tony Schermaier, massage therapists extraordinaire, for their skillful hands and listening hearts

My three daughters, Sue, Sandy, and Beth, for loving me and being open to my work

My parents, Don and Helen Resch, for all they taught me when they were here

All those who were open to receiving angel letters, and to those who allowed me to include their letters in this book

Those authors whose books have nourished me spiritually and helped me to become more open and willing to share my own spiritual challenges and growth

Down-to-Earth Angels

The loving angels who expressed themselves through the letters
My spiritual teachers, guides, and helpers
Archangel Michael, for his tremendous love, warmth, and encouragement

Introduction

The seed of belief in the existence of angels was planted in me when I was a child of perhaps four or five years of age. My maternal grandmother lived in an old house in East Cleveland. What hung in one of her spare bedrooms was awe-inspiring to my young eyes. The bottom of the picture was about eye level, and the top almost reached to the ceiling. Its frame was several inches wide, quite ornate and painted gold. It was the classic picture of the guardian angel protecting the children on the broken footbridge. I spent long periods staring at all the details of that huge painting. It touched my little child's heart. I found myself identifying with the children, the angel, and the footbridge.

This belief in angels was nourished by the guardian angel prayer I learned in my childhood catechism classes:

> Angel of God, my guardian dear,
> To whom God's love commits me here,
> Ever this day be at my side,
> To light, to guard, to rule and guide. Amen

Many years later, when I was teaching religion classes to grade school children, I was delighted that the prayer had been updated to language more appropriate for our times:

> Angel sent by God to guide me,
> Be my light and walk beside me,
> Be my guardian and protect me,
> On the paths of life direct me.

Prayer has always been important to me. I especially like simple—perhaps childlike—prayers. When my daughter Beth, now nineteen years old, was young, I wanted a simple morning prayer we could say together. Being fond of the rhythm of the prayer that begins, "Now I lay me down to sleep," I played with that rhythm and my own morning thoughts and wrote the following:

> Thank you, Lord, for this new day,
> Please bless all I do and say.
> Guide me as I work and play,
> Keep me close to You, I pray.

It is a prayer I continue to recite each morning as I wake from my slumber.

Just as simple prayers have always helped me feel connected to what I call God, or the Divine, or Love, or All That Is, so too nature has always given me that special feeling of Oneness. One afternoon in midsummer perhaps thirty years ago, I was sitting down at the small beach area of a little lake. My parents owned a cottage on this lake; and during my childhood and teenage years, I'd spent countless weekends enjoying it and its surroundings with my sisters, brother, and friends—swimming, canoeing, fishing and exploring. It was, and still is, a very magical place for my husband and me, our grown children, and our grandchildren. That particular afternoon so long ago, Spirit spoke to me; and the words I heard astonished me. First of all, I was amazed that Spirit spoke with such clarity. Secondly, God spoke through nature to give me a very important message.

I was evidently feeling a bit lonely or perhaps out-of-sorts, or simply wanted very much to know that God was close. I recall saying, "Lord, it's been so long since I've heard your voice. Please speak to me." The message was loving and distinct:

> You see my water and my trees,
> You feel my sun and my breeze,
> I speak to you through these things now
> As I have in times past—so, *enjoy!*

Those words have reverberated through my being so many, many times over the years. God spoke to me! God wanted me to enjoy all of creation! I was so totally, completely thrilled!

I suppose I, like so many others, have been searching all my life for meaning. All the reading, the renewals, the retreats, the workshops, the study groups, the times of intense prayer and meditation and so on have, of course, been helpful and have promoted spiritual growth. But what I'm finally beginning to appreciate is that more than anything, my mission in life is to allow myself to be truly happy, to allow myself to be truly joyful and to be the light that I am. What I am realizing is that I am happiest, most joyful and most full of light when I have the privilege of bringing happiness, joy and light to others. It is my hope to bring these to you, the reader, in greater measure through this work.

Although there are many angel offerings on the bookshelves, to my knowledge this book is unique in that it is primarily a compilation of "angel letters." Yes, I do relate my personal story of coming to know my angel, Marc, and how that relationship developed, as well as how the process of writing angel letters for others began and evolved. I also share experiences of continued personal spiritual growth and insight. I've told my stories as my way of coming out of what has been called by many the "spiritual closet." I've benefited greatly from other writers who have done the same, and hope that perhaps my openness will be an inspiration to you.

While I'm grateful for the opportunity to share, I am most grateful for the letters themselves. Eighty-one angel letters are included in this book. While each letter has deep personal meaning for the recipient, I believe that, collectively, they speak loudly to all of the nature of angels, and of their tremendous love, power, and longing to be of service.

It is my hope that those who are doubtful of the existence of angels but, nonetheless, willing to read these letters will become more receptive to the possibility of their existence. It is also my hope that those who believe in the existence of angels but are unaware of the possibility of angelic communication will be delighted to realize this is not only possible, but something for which the angels long! Yes, the angels want very much to be in touch with their charges! Finally, I believe there is much guidance and wisdom offered to all of us through these letters. Angels are manifestations of the Divine, sent to help us remember our divine nature. As such, they bring to us God's messages. The word angel means "messenger." The letters bring messages of peace, love, hope, joy, and more.

I truly wish I could offer you a blueprint for getting in contact with and communicating with your angel. This I cannot do. We each have our own ways of relating with our fellow human beings, with nature, animals, God, and All That Is. What I do offer to you is a sharing of the path I took—a path that required me to have the courage to be receptive to new ideas and possibilities. An angel intuitive opened the door. Communication through automatic writing brought much delight! Over time, and with patience and practice, I became more adept at discerning my angel's voice and guidance.

I believe this—a meaningful relationship with one's angel—is available to each and every one of us who truly desires it. It is certainly something your angel wants very much. Perhaps you, too, will want your own story to unfold and be willing to offer much hope and joy to others through its telling.

Listing of Recipients and Angels

indicates recipient's name has been changed

Date	Recipient	Angel	Angel's Essence *(listed if included in letter)*
9/03	Martha	T. J.	
9/5/03	Laura*	Tito	
9/7/03	Lydia*	Cecilia	
9/17/03	Betty	Mary Ellen	
9/17/03	Judy	Gloria	Openness to Asking
9/21/03	Sandy	Lexie	Power
9/24/03	Dan	McKilroy	Gentleness
9/24/03	Molly*	Leonardo	Compassion
9/24/03	Deirdre	Antoinette	Boldness
10/4/03	Henry	Germaine	Insightfulness
10/4/03	Sarah	Anita	Generosity
10/13/03	JoAnn	Lizzy	Vivaciousness
10/13/03	Barbara*	Cleo	Joy
10/16/03	Jamie	Julia	Tenderness
10/16/03	George	Pumpernickel	Laughter
10/16/03	Tari	Cupid	Naturalness
11/10/03	Diana	Sweet Pea	Cheerfulness
11/11/13	Judy	Jack	Energy
11/13/03	Cindy	Ethan	Genuineness
11/15/03	Candi	Angelina	Cuteness
12/1/03	Carol	Princess Diana	Loyalty
12/1/03	Kathleen	Giggles	Giggles

Down-to-Earth Angels

12/2/03	Kathleen	Simon	Trust
12/2/03	Kristin	Tinkerbell	Sweetness
12/7/03	Deborah*	Hardy	Speaking One's Truth
12/9/03	Mary Ann	Mary	Devotion
12/14/03	Lynne	Huckleberry	Adventurousness
12/14/03	Christine*	C. E.	Creative Expression
12/22/03	Amy	Jonathan	Reverence
12/23/03	Pam	Comforter	Comfort
12/26/03	Bob	Paul	Dedication
12/28/03	Cookie	Abigail	Peacefulness
12/29/03	Steve	Tony	Friendliness
1/2/04	Lois*	Suzanna	Freedom
1/4/04	Susan	Josephine	Motherliness
1/24/04	Libby*	Francine	Patience
2/1/04	Libby*	Francine	
2/15/04	Jennifer	Charles	Persistence
4/21/04	Beth	Christopher	Strength and Courage
5/22/04	Katie	Jezzebelle	Gaiety
5/24/04	Margaret*	J. J.	Calmness and Openness
5/28/04	Paula*	Glenda	Outspokenness
6/10/04	Noel	Henrietta	Love and Sweetness
6/14/04	Clar	Timothy	Assertiveness
6/23/04	Neal	Gregory	
6/28/04	Shar	Marianna	Cheerfulness and Trust
7/05/04	Mariah	Michael	Loving-Kindness
7/7/04	Beth	Annabelle	
7/15/04	Rochelle	Lisa	Light
7/20/04	Bill	Sir James	Tenacity
7/26/05	Tabitha	Maureen	Warmth of Heart
8/2/04	Richard	Sir Walter	Gallantry
8/3/04	Ginny	Angelic Trio	Joy
8/3/04	Tony	Graciela	
8/4/04	Marion*	Tina	Helpfulness
8/16/04	Jane	Heather	Organization

8/18/04	Cindy	Maxwell	Kindness
9/1/04	Christine	Leslie	
9/7/04	Gina	Belle	Beauty
9/8/04	Donna	Samantha	Healing
9/8/04	Stephanie	Connie	Simplicity
12/27/04	Kellie	Samuel	Joy in Doing
12/29/04	Mary Lou	Theresa	Longing
12/30/04	Barb	Daniel	Self-Starter
1/9/05	Marilyn	Tiffany	Gentleness
1/19/05	Tamara	Joseph	
1/19/05	Corky	Cynthia	
1/25/05	Lynne	Huckleberry	Adventurousness
1/25/05	Andrew	George	
2/4/05	Francesca	Colette	
2/4/05	Cindy	John	
2/4/05	Clar	Agnes	
2/13/05	Glenna	Hickory	
2/20/05	Tina	Jerome	
2/21/05	Dorothy	Thomas	
2/27/05	Scott	Bernard	
2/27/05	Alberta	Alicia	
4/2/05	Paula	Georgette	
4/2/05	Vince	Anthony	
4/12/05	Kim	Abigail	
4/18/05	Alan	Sir Raphael	

Chapter One

Across the Veil

That I am writing a book about angels comes as much of a surprise to me as to anyone. I consider it an honor and a joy, and undertake this task with the utmost honesty and humility. Angels are magnificent, loving beings who want the best for us. Each and every one of us has an angel; in fact, we each have many angels. It has been my experience, however, that it is best to get to know and work with one's primary angel before calling upon scores of other angels.

My first angelic experience occurred when I was a little girl, about seven or eight years old. It was our family custom to attend mass on Sundays and then come home and have breakfast together. One Sunday morning, before any other family members were awake, I decided to surprise my parents by setting the breakfast kitchen table "all by myself." As there were seven of us in our family, I needed to bring one chair from the dining room to the kitchen so there would be a seat for everyone. I remember walking into the dining room, putting both hands on the back of a chair, and then being unable to move. I asked myself, "Why am I standing here?" Yet I still could not move. Again I wondered, "Why am I standing here?" Just then I heard a loud crash in the kitchen. My mother came running and saw what had happened: the large glass overhead light had come loose and fallen. She explained that she had taken it down the day before to wash it and evidently had not secured it properly. After explaining my experience to her, she simply yet gratefully said, "Your angel was protecting you."

My angel now has a name. His name is Marc, and we are in close communication all the time. I have not always known his name, and have not always been consciously in touch with him. But I do know that he has been loving me, guiding me, and protecting me all my life. This relationship brings me great joy and happiness; and so I share my story with you.

Meeting My Angel

Over the years I've read hundreds of books, most of which fall into the personal or spiritual growth, new age, and health categories. For whatever reason, fiction has never been of much interest to me. Early in the year 2002, I voraciously read many of Doreen Virtue's books about angels and listened to several of her cassette tapes. In midsummer of that same year, I was reading a monthly newsletter written by Dr. Christiane Northrup, best-selling author of *Women's Bodies, Women's Wisdom* and *The Wisdom of Menopause,* in which she mentioned an angel intuitive by the name of Louise Cook. I felt very much inclined to call Louise to schedule a phone session and meet my angel through her. Louise is a dear, sweet woman in her eighties who resides in Maryland. In the first of my four phone sessions with her, she explained that she had been having a massage when the massage therapist told her that her angel was present and had a message for her. Her angel wanted Louise to know that if she wanted to communicate with her, she could do that. The massage therapist has not seen Louise's angel or anyone else's angel since that occurrence. Louise explained to me that she began to interact with her angel, and that over time she received the gift of being able to shift her energy, see other people's angels, and act as a mediator between others and their angels. I did not tape-record my sessions with Louise, but took as many notes as I could manage. These were very emotional encounters for me, and teardrops can certainly be found on the pages of my journal!

In my first session, Louise told me my angel was a male angel. She said, "The energy he brings is beautiful." Through Louise, he told me that I have the ability to be in charge of *everything* in my life, that there is a resistance when someone tells me what to do. He sees this resistance as being good, as it is my body or psyche saying no. She then described him physically: "He has a robe. He's so handsome and beautiful. He's about 5' 9" or 5' 10" tall. He's very male, with hair to his shoulders. His hair is neither dark nor blond. It's *beautiful* hair with highlights. Hair represents strength and femininity. He has dark eyes and beautiful thick lashes. His eyes are dark, and the darkness of eyes is important. Like the earth, like bark, dark-colored eyes represent strength."

As she looked into his eyes, she could see strength, as well as softness in that strength. She said his strength was like that of a mother's; one can feel both the strength and the softness. His simple white robe—white representing purity—was softly gathered at the shoulders. It was gathered at the waist as well, with a magic cord that brought together the earth and heaven. Louise went on to say that Marc wanted me to know that when I dance or listen to music, it is as spiritual as when I am praying. He told me that stress was keeping me from experiencing balance. He said, "Because you are so spiritual and grounded, you can be strong." My angel told me that I was very good at visualizing, and that whenever I wanted guidance or anything, I was to visualize him. Louise explained to me that angels aren't really named, but that they gladly take on a name, as we humans are more comfortable calling on someone who has a name. I really had no specific preference for his name, so he chose to be called "Marc." (I instinctively spelled his name with a *c,* perhaps because I've been a French teacher for some twenty-five years now.)

As the session continued, Marc said, "I'm your higher energy. At the beginning of your day, ask me to be like a snowplow—to smooth it out, and I will do that for you. When you want to know something, just ask and let it come in. Letting go is letting me do it. Give it up after the asking." I then asked Marc, "What is my divine purpose?" He responded, "Your divine purpose is to be happy! Enjoy! God is love! Happiness is strength! If everyone were happy, would there be any war? When anyone causes pain, that person is in pain. Energy matches energy. Like matches like. You know basically to be happy is God."

We went on to address some childhood wounds: how when I was growing up I never felt happy, accepted, or validated, and how I felt like a financial burden. The angels brought my father through (something Louise said is unusual) and through his tears he expressed that he was sorry and told me how much he loves and appreciates me. It was a blessed moment. Marc told me, "By your doing this, you are helping him, so when he is born again, he starts in a different place."

We then discussed a few more things: a persistent cough that concerned me; moving on after making mistakes; and how when I minimize the stress in my life, my aura would extend many, many miles further to positively affect others. He closed with, "Your life will never be boring. You'll meet exciting people. I want you to know that I adore you, and I am so privileged to have made this contact with you."

Over the course of the next few months, I had three more exchanges with Marc through Louise, each of them very special to me. In one session, he explained that I have five female angels with me all the time, but that he has access to hundreds of angels .He told me that if I had a question about my daughters, for example, he would turn to the female angels for direction and advice. He said he was here to help me get what I wanted. He gave his insights into world peace. We discussed some concerns I had pertaining to family members, diet, exercise, sex, health issues, and personal freedom. He said, "You are free. To please God is to be happy in your being." He told me he'd be available to guide me as much as I wanted, to keep my attention on what I wanted, and that a smile is a thousand times stronger than a hateful thought. He also told me something that brought great comfort: "Your mother is around you a lot, and is very happy. Your mom and dad are together." At the beginning of our fourth and final session, I asked Marc to please just talk to me, as opposed to me having to ask questions to which he'd respond. He explained that that was not the way angels worked. We must come to them with questions. I surmised that this has something to do with the fact that we each have a free will, which angels very carefully respect. They will never tell us what to do—but they are ever ready to love, guide, serve, and protect us.

During this last session with Louise, I told Marc that I believed this would be my last, and asked for his input. He simply stated, "Let it be an adventure." Somehow I intuited that Marc and I would be communicating on our own, that an intuitive would no longer be necessary. I told him that I wanted very much to hear his voice. Louise told me that she got goose bumps with his response; she said that goose bumps indicated that what was being said was very important. Marc told me, "Keep that desire in your awareness. The only reason you can't hear me is stress, fear, and so on. Say to yourself, 'You know, I think I'm going to hear you.' In the meantime, know that I have many other ways to communicate with you. I can lead you to that perfect dress, help with a car purchase, and soften a potential negative encounter." He went on to tell me to look for the joy in all situations, and that it is easy for me to be joyful because it is my nature.

Louise closed the session by saying, "He tells you he loves you and calls you his beautiful lady. He bows and leaves. But you know he never really leaves you." I wiped my tears, expressed my gratitude to Louise, hung up the phone, and sighed deeply.

Talking With Marc

Early in the fall of 2002, I again started to regularly write in a journal, something I'd done on and off over the years. Marc had become an important part of my life, and I often talked to him in my writings. I talked to him as one might talk to a best friend, or one's God, or anyone by whom one felt deeply loved. On September 19, 2002, I wrote, "I feel Marc's presence so much—his love, his guidance. Answers come almost as quickly as I ask them." I continued, "Marc, please show me how I can make my teaching at my school more meaningful to me so that I can be happy there."

I felt the urge to keep writing; it was as if my pencil wanted to write all by itself! It began by writing, "The way you can be happy is to have your morning to yourself. Take time to walk, to pray, and so on. The work will get done. Love yourself more. Say to yourself, I am a good teacher; my students love me and I love them. I am not afraid to discipline my students. It shows them I care when I do so. Each morning, remember to pray for your colleagues, and to thank God for all the benefits that come to you and your family from this employment."

I quivered with delight. My angel had just written to me through automatic writing! I thanked Marc for what had just appeared in my journal. Yet there was a part of me that doubted we were really communicating. There was a part of me that thought it was possibly a fanciful imagination. There was so much evidence that this relationship was real; and I found so much joy in the love, the guidance, and now the written communication. However, I wanted some kind of validation. It came shortly after.

The Ursuline Sophia Center

In September of 2002, I attended my first Spirit Seed Institute weekend at the Sophia Center of Ursuline College in Pepperpike, Ohio. Approximately twenty of us, two of whom were our teachers, met one full Saturday and Sunday per month for nine months. What an adventure—albeit difficult at times—in spiritual growth! The Institute did, in fact, do what it promised it would do: respond to our heart's longing for deeper spiritual connection, healing, and expression. I continue to feel grateful for those weekends, the growth I experienced, and the friendships that were cultivated.

That first weekend at the Sophia Center, I met Martha, sweet Martha. As we sat on the grass enjoying lunch, she mentioned a woman by the name of Mary Ellen Lucas, with whom she had had a "heart-healing" session. As Martha talked a bit, I simply knew I'd have to meet Mary Ellen and have a heart-healing session with her myself.

Heart Healing

My first session with Mary Ellen took place on October 8, 2002. In her sweet, gentle way, Mary Ellen entered my heart and helped me to do the same. I felt as if I had failed someone. She helped me to realize that I felt as if I'd failed myself. I felt that I should have been doing more to help others, specifically to help others heal. She helped me to see that I was being hard on myself, and I left her office feeling more whole, and more loving and accepting of myself.

Wanting to continue the process of healing my heart, I scheduled a second appointment for the following week. I asked Marc to be present and to interject his thoughts, if he felt it was appropriate. During the session, I shared with Mary Ellen some past issues between my deceased parents and myself that were still causing my heart to feel weary. With her help and guidance, I was able to forgive my parents for long-ago hurts. At one point, Mary Ellen's face brightened, and she laughed. (This special woman has the most delightful sense of humor!) She told me that my angel was present.

and that he wanted me to know that he spells his name the way I do in my journal—with a *c*. (Yeah! The validation I had longed for!) She added, "He's quite a character." To this I replied, "I know!" (More on this later.)

Toward the end of that session, Marc told Mary Ellen that I needed to learn to receive: that I was very good at giving, but that I needed to be open to asking for what I needed and to receiving it. Mary Ellen suggested that with Marc's help, I should ask, "What makes me happy? What gives me pleasure? What am I passionate about?" That night I wrote in my journal, "So, Marc, I'm putting these questions out there. You've told me to say, 'Come on, guys! Come on!' Help me answer these questions. I love you, Marc."

Letters from Marc

For many months, Marc wrote to me. He *is* quite a character. His letters made me laugh out loud. He'd tell me jokes, tell me to lighten up, and sing songs—ones about sunshine. Once he told me that being my angel all these years has sometimes been difficult for him, because I was so-o-o serious. He said it was good I had my husband, Rich, in my life to keep things light, and that without Rich my life would have been like one long, boring church service. (Ouch!) Yes, yes, yes, Marc has brought so much joy to my life. (Just now as I'm writing, he said, "And you've brought so much joy to *my* life, Donna!")

After many months of writing letters to me, Marc suggested I simply talk to him. He implied that writing all of our communications simply wasn't necessary. I wasn't sure if I was willing to give up the writing. As Mary Ellen told me in one of our many sessions that were to follow over the next year or so, "Writing things down helps to make the ethereal world concrete for you." This was true. Somehow seeing it in writing helped to make it more real. Eventually, though, after about a year, the written communications gave way to more frequent Spirit communication, something with which I now find myself very comfortable. And as a friend with whom I was having a massage last week said, "It's much more time efficient!" How true. How true. Yet the written communications were most necessary for me at the time, and I treasure those letters.

Marc and I had been relating to one another through Louise, through letter writing and through Spirit communication for approximately one year, when the angel of one of my twin daughters wrote to me. The letter came on July 10, 2003. Perhaps it shouldn't have come as such a surprise. Sue had met her angel, Josephine, through Louise Cook shortly after I met Marc. Sue and she had been in close touch, and Josephine had been such a comfort to her for some time.

Leah Rose

On May 20, 2003 Sue had given birth to a beautiful baby girl, Leah Rose. Leah Rose was born with Edward's Syndrome, also known as Trisomy 18, a rare genetic disorder. In the hospital, Sue and her husband, Jim, were gently told that Leah would most likely not live to be a year old. Our sweet little Leah was with us for eleven weeks. She was a joy to hold, exuded great love and, as will be expressed in Josephine's letter to Sue (Josephine always calls her "Susan"), Leah fulfilled her life's mission and is now working diligently on the other side of the veil.

I often talked to Josephine as we all cared for Leah and each other. Although Sue shared some of their conversations with me, I had not heard her angel's voice, nor expected to. I simply took comfort in knowing that she and Sue were close.

On July 11, 2003 Mary Ellen and I met. My heart held concern for Sue and Jim and their young son, Tyler, as well as concern for family members of a friend, Shirley, who had recently died. I also wanted to be open to whoever might want to come through Mary Ellen to me, knowing full well that whoever appeared to me would want only the best for me.

After we prayed silently, Mary Ellen began, "Who comes to you first is St. Michael. He's not saying much, but it is being acknowledged that you are connecting with him—his courage, his strength, his protection. He's the one you're to go to. Your angel is acknowledging this."

I laughed and explained to Mary Ellen that recently I had been turning to Michael. (He had asked me to call him "Michael," as opposed to the more formal "Archangel Michael.") Sometimes I felt torn, as if I were slighting Marc. Marc had been teasing me, as if to say, "Oh, so I'm not good enough any more!" Marc also told me some of the female angels were correcting him on this, telling him that I might not understand, might not realize he was simply joking. "Well," continued Mary Ellen. "Michael is up here behind you and Marc is down here, to the side. Marc is giving the deference to Michael."

Josephine's Message

She then asked if I knew a woman whose name began with a "J." "It's Julia, or Georgianna, or Josephine. Do you know a Josephine?"

"Not personally," I replied. "She's an angel. She's Sue's angel."

"Yes, because I'm getting that she's an angel."

Mary Ellen expressed surprise that Josephine would come in for me when she's my daughter's angel. "Josephine wants you to know that Susan is better than you think."

"May I ask her a question?"

"Sure," answered Mary Ellen.

"Yesterday, Josephine wrote me a letter."

"Yes, yes. In your own hand? This is what she says: It was in your own hand. Yes, that was from her."

"Good," I replied. "Then I was not imagining it."

"No. She says it was automatic writing; that's a term I would understand. She says you can do that with any of them."

"I do that all the time with my angel, but I had never done that with another angel."

Mary Ellen continued. "She says, 'Oh, yes, you can do that with any of them.'"

"What do you mean—any of them?"

"Very simply, you can do that with any of them."

I then asked, "Do I need to know their name? For example, if I wanted my brother Bill's angel to write to me…"

"She says that the name is important to you."

"Yes, it is."

"Josephine is saying to me that names are not that important to angels, but it is for you, so you can ask who it is. She says for you to ask the name first, because you need that. If you were to start writing and not know who was speaking to you, you would not be comfortable."

Mary Ellen said she did not know why Josephine was the one talking, as she was not my angel. I explained that I'd been praying to Josephine a lot recently out of concern for my daughter, Sue. Leah was now about seven weeks old. She was at home with her family for some time now, being gravity-fed through a tiny tube in her nose that led to her stomach. I acknowledged Josephine speaking to me for the first time a couple days prior, when she had said to me, "Please stop worrying about Susan. You're interfering with what we're trying do."

"Right," responded Mary Ellen.

"Sue told me that Leah's angel's name is Christine. So as a result of that, I've been praying to both of their angels. The connection with Josephine is very, very new to me."

"So maybe that is why she's talking so much…which is good."

"It is good. It's wonderful," I commented.

Mary Ellen continued. "She's letting me know that you can do this on any of the angelic levels, you just don't know it. I guess this question is more for me, but have you always been sort of plugged in with angels, or drawn to angels?"

"Probably. I remember having a very protective incident when I was a child. So I've always believed in angels."

"All right. She is kind of letting me know that the place where you really are peaceful and comfortable is in the angelic realms. There's order in angels, she says. That's why whom we would call St. Michael is given higher respect, greater due. The archangels are powerful."

"I've been calling on them much more lately," I commented.

"This is good. She wants you to do this. They are very powerful. You do not want to **not** call on them."

Josephine, through Mary Ellen, then spent some time talking to me about burdens I was carrying for family members. She explained the difference between a burden and a responsibility, and said that the sense of burden could be lifted as I carried out my responsibilities by asking the angels for help. Josephine said, *"The asking is important."*

There was then a long pause.

Mary Visits

Mary Ellen then spoke. "Mary comes in for you. I knew she was going to come. (I started to cry, but then composed myself, as I wanted to hear everything Mary Ellen had to say.) She shows herself holding Leah. Mary says, 'She is my baby. She is my baby, and she is held.'"

Mary Ellen said, "Leah is wrapped in this beautiful, white blanket. It looks like a christening blanket. I'm asking if she has a blanket like this, and she's telling me 'no.' It is so very heavenly; it's got little mother of pearls all throughout. It's like the finest material. I don't know how to describe it. It's really beautiful. Leah is wrapped in this and Mary holds her. She says that you are to know that Leah is held and she is held by her." Mary tells you, 'When you hold her, she is held by me. When her mother holds her, she is held by me. When her father holds her, she is held by me. When your husband holds her, she is held by me.'" I started to cry again. Mary Ellen waited for me to quiet myself and then said, "I have to say, Donna, that is probably the most I've heard Mary talk."

I responded, "Oh, my."

"Yes, said Mary Ellen. "She usually doesn't talk that much. She usually comes in and says hello, and then leaves." I asked, "What if none of us is holding Leah?" Through Mary Ellen, Mary responded, "She is held. She's always held by me. And when she is not held by one of you, angels are around her as well."

Josephine Returns

I continued to wipe my tears and listen. A short pause followed. Mary had left and Josephine had returned. Josephine said, "Yes, this is a cross to bear. But do you not feel your heart soften when you are with Leah?"

"Absolutely. We all do," I responded.

"You earthlings often do not think that little ones such as she are teachers of wisdom, and yet she is. There is not one who has not been affected by her, and that includes people at the hospital, in the delivery room, in the nursery. Everybody was affected."

Mary Ellen went on, "Josephine is saying that she wants to answer your questions, and she wants you to know that she's the one who will answer them. Your angel Marc is here. You know that. And your guides are here, but they're staying back. She's the person being directed today to answer. She is wanting me to tell you what I was thinking about this morning around you. She's telling me to use my own words. The growth I've seen in you, Donna, is phenomenal."

"It is phenomenal," I responded.

"People don't change as quickly as you have, and I know it hasn't been easy for you. But I feel like there's been such a huge growth and evolution for you. It's really, really awe-inspiring. I was wanting to tell you that."

"I am aware of this. I am very grateful for it. I just feel like it's heaven coming in here to kind of move me along. And I want to thank Josephine…for everything. For being Sue's angel. Sue loves her very much."

"My sense of Josephine is that she's very calm, very peaceful or sedate, very sweet and reassuring, almost in a motherly way, but not overbearing. She's very different from your angel." (We both laughed!)

The Council

I will not go into all the details of the remainder of this session, mainly because it does not pertain directly to angels. Perhaps it is sufficient to mention that I told Mary Ellen that I kept hearing the word *we.* As I found myself often wondering who was talking to me, Marc suggested I ask, "Who's 'we'?" at this session.

Mary Ellen looked and listened. I was told that I have a council of fifteen who work over me, who oversee me. They love and want the best for me. They watch, see me falter, and see me grow. Marc is directed by them. They told me I had a main task to do, which was not being made clear at that time. Mary Ellen told me that an ancient male energy was saying to me, "You are loved and honored, and you are a rarity in how you have moved powerfully into your divine self. You are blessed…and that is all."

I replied, "That's enough. That's a lot." I told myself I'd try to process all of that later.

The remainder of our time together was spent being in touch with my friend, Shirley, who had recently died and whose family was grieving. I made a copy of that portion of the tape and passed it on to them. Shirley is well.

If you, my dear reader, have followed most of what you've just read, my hat is off to you. There were times when I felt as if I were just along for the ride. I know I'm a very sane person, and trust God and God's guidance with a passion. But I must admit things were happening so fast, well—it just got confusing at times. Nevertheless, I forged ahead.

A Letter for Martha

Josephine had told me I had access to all the angels. She had told me that I plug into the angelic realms as easily as one might push an electrical plug into an outlet.

Shortly after receiving Josephine's letter, other family members' angels wrote as well. There were perhaps six or seven letters. My daughter, Sue, and I also became aware that we were "picking up" the same angel names for family members. It was exciting for us, and I was so appreciative that this "new gift" of mine was understood and accepted by family.

Early in September of 2003, I was sharing my angel letter writing with Martha, my Spirit Seed Sister who had introduced me to Mary Ellen. As we closed our phone conversation, she said, "If you ever hear from my angel, please let me know." I laughed, almost as if to say, "Who knows what's going to happen next?" and told her I'd let her know if I got anything. As I hung up the phone, I felt the presence of a male angel. Feeling compelled to write, I immediately went up to my bedroom and began to write in my journal. Approximately a half-hour later, I called Martha and excitedly told her that I had a letter for her from her angel. I asked if she wanted me to read it to her, and she responded, "Absolutely!" Here is the letter I received:

Dear Donna,

There truly is nothing for you to worry about when you communicate with us angels. We want what is the very best for you and those you love. You are concerned about "human error," your imagination taking over, etc. These concerns could be true and valid, but in your case, you have indeed been, as you say, given a gift. We have permission from the most high to communicate with you whenever you ask. You are "labeled" very trustworthy, very good, very worthy.

The bond that you share with my beloved Martha is indeed a deep one—deeper than either one of you realize. It is a bond that will be strengthened over time and is not to be taken lightly. You are, in a very real sense, soul sisters and have known each other in past lives—multiple lives—and it is not by chance that you meet again at this time.

Leah did indeed offer strength to Martha when she needed it. Leah is connected to your heart, and you can ask her for her help whenever you like. She appreciates all the love and care you gave her and her parents during her short time on earth. As Martha said, more will unfold.

My name is indeed Timothy James (T. J., if you will). Please do tell this to Martha. It can wait until next Friday.

Tell her I like my name—especially T. J.—and that I look forward to working with her more closely. In fact it is something I've been longing for—as you earthlings would say. She does carry many, many burdens for others, and there is much that I can do to help her. May you both be richly blessed. You are deeply blessed by us all. Thank you for being brave, for trusting me and all of us on this side of the veil. You can call on me, too, you know. Marc and I are good buddies. We both like your "human" expressions. We share them, compare them, talk and laugh about them. I'm glad I have you as a friend now, too.

T. J. was talking in a fast-paced, upbeat manner, and I could tell he was going to go on for a while. So, I telepathically asked him, "T. J., do you like to talk?"

I **love** to talk—to anyone who will listen. Marc is actually quite a good listener. He likes to laugh. I like to joke and talk. So, you might say we "make a pretty good team." Marc is always "rooting for you." We like that expression—"rooting for you." It's so uplifting. Encouragement is one of the greatest forms of love, as you know.

Yes, I could go on and on. You might even say I should go to Talkers Anonymous because I go on and on and on. Thanks for listening. This has been very special to me. I like the word "special," as do you. It covers so many different scenarios. Now "scenarios"—that's a neat word if you think about it. Scenes—so many scenes—in our lives, in our minds. And boy, you and I can create scenarios in our minds and—poof!—we can bring that scenario alive in our lives.

You humans are just *so, so* powerful. It's really amazing (great phrase!) that you don't use your power more. It can be so much fun! But you all hold back so much—like somebody's going to yell at you. But nobody's going to yell. In fact, people will admire you, and you can do so much good.

So, anyway, now that I've talked your ears off (cute expression, huh?)—hey, again, thanks! Please, oh please, be in touch. I'd love that—and Marc is just fine with it, too. Your hubby ☺, by the way, is a swell guy. And his angel, Sir Walter, well, he's the best, too. So-o-o, good night, my love, sleep tight, and don't let the bedbugs bite.

Timothy James (Oh, how formal!)

T. J.

Receiving Angel Letters

And so the process of receiving and passing on angel letters began. Of course, the letters in this book are all included with the permission of the recipients. A few of the first names have been changed to preserve privacy, and those changes have been indicated with an asterisk. A small number of those who received letters chose not to have their letters included. I stressed to all that whether to include one's letter in the book and whether to change one's name were very personal, individual decisions that would be honored. I am grateful to all who were open to receiving letters, and to all who allowed their letters to be published. None of the angels' names have been changed! (I just love their names! I just heard, "We love them, too, Donna!")

This past July (2004), I sent a note to angel letter recipients explaining that I believed the time had come for the letters to be complied into a book. If anyone wanted to have his or her response to the letter included in the book, that response would be most welcome. This process has been ongoing. Letters have been written for friends, family members, neighbors, healthcare professionals, colleagues, friends of friends, people I've met very casually, and people I've never met. This has all been quite an unexpected adventure in my life!

An Angel Essence

As you read the letters, you will notice that many of them refer to the angel's essence. Identifying the angel's essence came about as a result of a session I had with Mary Ellen, shortly after writing the first four letters (excluding the first few letters received for family members.)

I said to Mary Ellen, "Perhaps the angelic realm can help me to understand something that I've been grappling with. That is, I've heard that people's angels are their higher selves. Is this true?"

Mary Ellen told me that although Marc was present, it would be the council who would be addressing me on this question. They began by telling me that if I were to read about the angelic realms, I would find that most of what has been written is not valid, and that most of my information would come largely from my own experiences. "It is important that you write down your experiences, as that helps to make them tangible for you," they reminded me.

They then helped me to better understand the relationship of a person to his or her angel. Each person's primary angel is chosen for him or her based on the angel's essence and the person's highest potential. "The angel that a person has as her own personal angel is her higher self, from the understanding that this is the potential that can be reached."

To help me understand, the council continued by giving me examples. "For instance, what is it about your angel Marc that is an encouragement, and that shows a potential for you that is an important inspiration or message only for you?" (I thought a moment but truly did not know how to respond.) They responded, "He brings humor. He brings joy. He brings wisdom, but he is known more for his lightness of being. Is that not something that you strive for? Is that not something that is in the depths of you that you can bring to others? Do you see how that works?"

I thought a moment and then replied, "Hmmmm...Do I see how that works? I've often wondered. I can see his joy, his lightness, and his humor. He's so fun to be around, and I'm so-o-o-o serious."

Mary Ellen asked, "What's the message for you, Donna?"

"I don't know how to put it into words. It's like I'd have to do a big flip-flop!"

"Yes, but we're always striving."

"So maybe that's kind of a goal for me—to let go of some of the heaviness and seriousness."

Mary Ellen laughed gently. "Donna, if you're plugging into the angelic realms, there's a lot of joy there!"

I couldn't help but exclaim, "Oh, but I want to take this all so seriously!"

Mary Ellen continued. "So they want to give you another example. They're asking about Susan's angel. What would you say is the essence of her angel?"

"Caring, loving, motherly..."

"Yes, motherly. The angel that stands by her shows what is in Susan, and what can be drawn out that's already there, except she doesn't always see it. Is Susan to be mother in the most beautiful sense of the word? Yes. She has a mother's heart. She has a mother's presence. It is a goal for her to move into the potential of who she is.

"You will see when you tell others about their angels. These angels are carefully chosen for each person. It is the person's task to learn what they can to emulate. There is comfort offered. There is guidance offered. But most importantly, there is inspiration of what a person can be. And you will see that."

My new understanding of the importance of an angel's essence was immediately incorporated into the angel letters. I found this exciting! Knowing my angel's essence was helpful to me. I was happy to be able to tell others not only their angel's name, but also their angel's essence. Many times, although sometimes not, the angels simply stated their essence.

Logic 101 also kicked in for me. If my highest potential could be reached by growing into the essence of my angel, then it would behoove me to put the intention out into the Universe to do just that. Perhaps it suffices to say that the Universe has generously responded to my intention, and I am finding I live with a lighter heart and greater joy with each passing day. (Thank you, God, and Marc!)

The Angels Minister to Me

A few more thoughts before I turn the letters and responses over to you, dear reader. After I wrote a few letters in my journal and then transferred them onto the computer, the angels suggested I simply write "automatically" directly onto the computer. They were pleased I was open to their suggestions. This process was much more time-efficient.

Also, I was very anxious for the angel letters to be addressed to the person for whom the message was intended, as opposed to me. But the angels had it their way! For several months after the letters began, the angels insisted on addressing the letters to me, and ministered to me through the letters. They lovingly led me to the place where I was finally comfortable and confident with my gift and my work.

My hope is that sharing this deeply personal story will be of value to all of you who are on your own spiritual paths. I love God, all the angels, my teachers and guides, and all of you. Blessed be and so it is!

Chapter Two

Angel Letters

September 5, 2003

Dear Donna,

I'd really rather say, "Hello, Donna," but protocol requires I say, "Dear Donna," in a letter. So you think you have the ability to call upon anybody's angel, do you? Well, what makes you so special? Well, I'll tell you. It's God himself (I realize that's not politically correct—God himself or herself) that has told us we must comply and to communicate with you when you call upon us to do so.

So, you love Laura*, as do I. There is so much I can do to help her. But you see, she doesn't ask. That is the problem. That, and she's also very stubborn. Well, I can be stubborn too. But hey, all things are possible with God, right? So now that she knows my name (she did seem to like it, I'm happy to say), I think things are going to happen. But please do say a little prayer. I'd really like nothing more than to have a central role in her life. She has so, so much love inside of her, and so many gifts. If she'd just call upon me—like, "Hey, Tito"—well, that would be music to my ears.

There's really nothing I wouldn't do for that woman. We'd make a great team—a great healing team as well as a great laughing team. You see, I like to laugh now and again. But not all the time. You might say I'm rather hard-nosed. Yup, that's kind of my nature. But I do have a very, very big heart. I love hugs and words of love. So, please, if you would, don't let my terseness put you off. Please pass this on to Laura. I'd really like for us to work together closely. You might say I fear her rejection a little. So her open arms would do a whole lot for me. I hope she and I can work together. Again, please say a little prayer.

A tough angel to love, yes. But I **am** loveable.

Tito

Down-to-Earth Angels

September 7, 2003

Dear Donna,

Now didn't you and Lydia* have a *fun* day together? Yes, Lydia was absolutely correct: It **was** meant to be! Please don't be so nervous. I know this is different for you to just pick up a pencil and start writing—just switching from reading about essential oils to—oh my, I almost forgot Cecilia was going to write to me.

I am so very pleased that Lydia had a chance to share the tough times she's had for so long with you. You are definitely to be trusted—with all she had to tell you, including her desires to have John* be a bigger part of her life. **I did** whisper in your ear that John's* angel (Agnes, yes, you did hear correctly earlier today) and I can work together on this relationship. Please do not be so nervous. And, you do not have to share this with Lydia until you are ready.

You have, my dear, taken on a big responsibility—to talk to all of us angels. And we all see that you want to be of service to others. But you must also have fun with this whole process. Oh my, if all of life were work and seriousness, how dull and full of drudgery it would be! How often have you heard Lydia use the word *fun?* Yes, very often. That's why she's so quick to smile and a delight to be with. She's enjoying her life, and we all feel—well, it's about time! Well, we want you to have fun, too. So, relax, enjoy, and, as Marc, your special angel, has told you time and time again, "Let it be an adventure."

We love you.

Cecelia

September 17, 2003

Dear Donna,

Believe me, we are all learning. This is the first time you've written an angel letter for someone you've never met—my dear, sweet Betty (Aunt Betty to your dear, sweet Martha!). And this is the first time I've communicated to Betty in this form. Believe you me; I am so excited this opportunity has come about. I love Betty so much. And, actually, we have worked together quite closely all these years. She does love me and is aware of my presence. But there's that doggone thin veil that still separates your world from the angelic realm. It will be lifting soon, though; and, oh! what a glorious time it will be!

Actually, we angels are having more fun than we've had in our entire lives! We've been given the "go ahead," you might say, to come into contact with our humans in any way that they are open to.

Yes, Betty and I have been working together for a long time. There is more for us to do, though. And this short communication and her familiarity with my name are going to open the door for us to get to know each other very well.

Oh my, what a sweet, sweet soul she is. Open to the mysteries of the universe. Curious about all the goings on in the Spirit world. Yes, open is a good word to describe her. That's why this letter is being written. She is so open to it. So many gifts she has, and such a **huge** heart!

I'm delighted we've made this contact. We in the angelic realm know you're still a little nervous about your new gift. But lots of confirmation will come your way that you might step out fearlessly and boldly on our behalf.

We all love you, and I love my Betty so very, very much. Words cannot describe this love I feel. But it feels good to try to put it into words.

Mary Ellen

Betty responded to her letter:

Dear Donna,

What a surprise! I know you will understand my delight and eagerness to reply when I read Mary Ellen's message to you. What a happy, loving Spirit!

Thank you! Thank you! I wonder how many years I have hovered on the verge of what you are doing—wanting very much to communicate—feeling a welcome, but hesitating—standing there, pigeon-toed—too shy to knock on the door.

With that joyful, loving letter, I shall put aside my shyness and let her take me by the hand. After reading it, I racked my memory to see whether I had known a Mary Ellen. I couldn't think of one who had really been a part of my life. Then it came to me! I had a doll I called Mary Ellen. I had other dolls—more glamorous (with real hair and long-lashed eyes that opened and closed.) But it was Mary Ellen I loved—and I can still see her chubby cheeks and smile.

A big hug of thanks,

Betty

PS, I kept her name covered until the very end of her letter.

In the following letter, the angels tell me they are pleased that I am open to their suggestions. Up to this point, I had been writing the letters in my journal and then typing them onto the computer. They helped me realize that I could write "automatically" using the keyboard, something I hadn't considered before their input.

September 17, 2003

Dear Donna,

You are going to find that this type of letter writing is most efficient, and we in the angelic realm are most pleased that you are open to our suggestions.

Yes, I did very much want to get in touch with my beloved Judy in this special way. I really have been longing and trying to reach her for some time, but to no avail. Now that she knows my name and has this letter, perhaps things will progress more quickly.

As you know, the Spirit world brought the two of you back together at this time. You both have so much to offer to each other. For one thing, you are both very comfortable with each other—something that is not to be taken lightly. Another thing you have in common is your desire to be healers in the truest sense of the word—healers of the heart. The heart, as you know, is your connecting link to the God of the Universe and to your higher self. Your hearts are connected in a very deep way. Even if you should part ways, the heart connection will always be there.

It is so important that Judy hears once again that she must **ask** me to help, to guide her, to show her, to speak to her—whether through her inner listening or through writing. Perhaps she can even put up little notes around her house, in her car, etc., just as reminders that I am always with her and would love to work very closely with her. These are just some ideas, which I would never impose upon her, but which I'm feeling she might be open to at this time.

More than anything, I want her to know how much I love her and how much I want her highest good for her. She is such an angel! ☺ Always being so concerned about others. It is also important for her to extend to herself the same considerations she offers to others…(I feel I'm being a bit forward here.) But please tell Judy through this communication that deep within her is this ability to ask for what she needs, to make her desires be made known to the Universe, and that the Universe would love nothing more than to send to her her heart's desires, of which she is so, so very deserving. Oh, the love and healing she has given to others—far beyond what she is aware of! We on this side want her to receive an abundance of love and healing in return. Yes, you are right. In my essence I am open to receiving and to asking for what it is I need. (Yes, we angels have needs, too.) And yes, this quality is something for which Judy might strive in order that she might reach her highest potential.

We all love you (meaning you and Judy) so very, very much. We will be in touch, in any manner to which you are open. We are always, always with you and love our "work." You are our delight.

Gloria and the Angelic Realm

Judy's response to her letter:

Dear Donna,

Thank you so much for this beautiful, affirming letter. Asking for others has never been difficult for me, but it has always been difficult for me to ask for myself. Because of

Donna Allen

your wonderful angel letter, it has become easier to ask for myself. I treasure our relationship and feel so blessed that the Universe reunited us. With love, Judy

When I asked my daughter, Sandy, if she'd like a letter from her angel, she was very nervous and hesitant. She said she'd like me to write a few lines and then let her read them to see if she wanted me to continue. *I* knew there was nothing to be afraid of, but *she* didn't. During a session with Mary Ellen, this issue was brought up. Sandy's angel wanted to write a letter for her, thus I received the "go ahead" referred to in Sandy's letter, but her angel did not want me to write a shortened version. What follows is the letter.

September 21, 2003

Dear Donna,

It seems like I've been waiting a long time to write this letter. I know it's only been a few days since you got the go ahead from Mary Ellen, but a few days can be a long time, even for an angel.

So, you know my essence—Power! Yes, Power is my essence and the highest potential for your beloved daughter, Sandy. I am going to refer to her as Sandy because that is what she is most comfortable with. It is good that you asked about my essence, as that gives you a better understanding of and appreciation for Sandy.

Sandy is indeed powerful and is using that power to help many, many people. In some ways she is using that power for herself, too; but she will be using her power in increasing measure to help herself in the coming year. This is something that is long overdue. She must learn to put some of her own needs first, before the needs of others. This is not selfish. This is what one must do to reach her highest potential. Each person's soul and body deserves the highest respect and care. It is the individual who must give this to him or herself.

Yes, your daughter has a huge heart. **Huge!** It is my hope that she will open her heart to herself. She needn't be afraid of doing so. You know how difficult it has been for you to open your own heart. It takes Courage—with a capital *C*. So much of the past surfaces when the heart opens. So much forgiveness, toward one's self and toward others, is called for. It is natural to scream, "Why should I forgive him/her?" And yet, it is for your own well-being that one forgives. Whatever one holds inside which is less than love affects one's well-being, which in turn affects all of those around you. That is why the Good Shepherd stressed the need to forgive and to love others **as you love yourself.** So many in your poor, stressed world do not take the precious time that is needed to love themselves…so much scurrying, so much hurrying.

As you know, great changes are taking place upon the face of the earth. But there is great hope…great hope. We in the angelic realm are so pleased with your work. You were born to do this work, as you are learning. We love you so, and we love so very much those that you love. Go forth with courage and power. You can ask for my help, guidance, and comfort whenever you wish, and I will rush to your side, as I will do for your Sandy.

Peace and great love,

Alexandra (Lexie)

(whichever name Sandy prefers)

Sandy responded to her letter approximately fourteen months after receiving it:

Dear Mom,

For some reason, I find it easier to talk to my angel Lexie than to God. I'm very comfortable talking to her in a casual manner. I might say, "Help, Lexie," or "What's going on?" She just seems very "human" to me. This relationship has opened the spiritual world to me in a new way. I find myself relying on spiritual help and guidance more than ever before.

Two things really stood out for me in my letter—that my angel's essence is power and that I have a huge heart. I've found that as I've opened my heart more to others, I've also opened my heart much more to myself.

It's very important to me to fight for my rights and for the rights of others and to help others as much as possible. My growing relationship with Lexie, and opening my heart to others as well as myself, has given me courage and hope to continue my daily work. Love, Sandy

September 24, 2003

Dear Donna,

You are starting to see that the reason we are addressing these letters to you is that you have work to do, my dear, and we want to give you all the support you need! You will not be shortchanged in this process, we promise you that! Yes, we love you very much. Yes, we love Dan very much. And we are so happy that the two of you have met and that a level of deep trust has developed so quickly. We hated to disturb your sleep, but we knew that you needed to hear that you were **perfectly** safe with Dan. You have also seen that as that healing took place, a healing took place in your relationship to **all** men. We stress the word "all" because your Goliath experience was necessary for you to be in the place you are now.

You feel awkward that we are talking so much to you in these letters. That is as it must be for quite a while, and there is a purpose to it that you will understand in due time. So, you have passed on Dan's angel's name and you have passed on his essence. Yet, you feel this is not enough. Yet, we tell you that this is enough at this time.

McKilroy is Gentle, with a capital *G*. He is very strong, somewhat shy in his own way, which is why he is not speaking at this time. But he will be in touch with Dan, don't you worry. He is kind, sweet…and oh, so gentle. He and Dan will be developing a very strong bond, something that will be beneficial to them both. He is simply telling us to say "hi" to Dan. He also loves him very much, but we're adding that on our own.

We're happy that your spirits have picked up now that you've heard from Deirdre, our sweetheart as well as Dan's! We'll be in touch. We love you!

The Angelic Realm

September 24, 2003

Dear Donna,

Thanks for taking the time to write. We all know that you aren't feeling all that well and that you are trying to keep your priorities in the correct order, as advised by your guides and teachers. It is so important that you trust the timing of the universe and not put pressure on yourself. Remember, the angelic realm is full of joy! Yes, we are anxious to write to our "humans," as you call them. We call them by name with each other, and we automatically know when we are referring to a human.

Yes, my name is Leonard (pronounced as in Leonardo da Vinci, without the *o*). Leo is just fine with me, too. And yes, you heard correctly. My essence is one of strength and compassion. Compassion—oh, how I love the sound of that word and all that it encompasses. It is often the strongest connecting link between human souls. And it often takes great strength to allow that connection to be made. Actually, compassion (a pal to love) and strength must go hand in hand. One cannot exist without the other. This is something to think about.

Do not be afraid! Have compassion for yourself. This is something that my Molly* must do for herself also. She must have much compassion for herself. There is a lack in this area. The strength is there. The compassion is there. The strength and compassion of which I speak are deep within her. We can work together to bring their presence to her awareness and to greater expression.

So, perhaps you do not trust this process fully yet. You still feel as if you are faltering—that your steps are faltering. But do not be afraid. We can give you the courage you need to do your work. We are all working on this side to bring

Down-to-Earth Angels

you to the place you need to be in order to do your work with joy and peace. You are not alone. Molly is not alone. Not one human being on planet Earth is alone. Each one of us was carefully chosen for each one of you. We need you!

So, be of good cheer. Pass this message on to Molly, whom I love dearly. We will become good friends; I just know it. Peace. Love. Joy.

Leonard (Leo)

September 24, 2003

Dear Donna,

So, you and Deirdre are in full swing. That's what Deirdre is—a swinger. She is letting herself fly, and we are so much enjoying her ride. She is so very gifted, so full of life, so courageous and so loving. What a daring combination! We actually take inspiration from her, something you humans might find difficult to understand.

We would like to state something that you and Deirdre already know. Nothing happens by chance. Your meeting at the Sophia Center was not by chance. The bond that has developed between you and Deirdre, and between you and Dan, and so on is not by chance. What we would like to say is that we delight in these relationships!

Donna, we would like to honor your desire, although unspoken, that we speak to Deirdre, whom you love. Deirdre, we would just like to tell you that we are so very pleased with all of the love you are extending to others. You are bold in your expression of love and caring. What a beautiful use of boldness! To be able to say, "I love boldly," is so beautiful; it makes us in the angelic realm want to cry. Oh, how your poor world needs people who are not afraid to love boldly. Please know you can turn to any and all of us whenever you need guidance, courage, strength, or peace. We will gladly give all this to you and more. Know that the essence of your angel, Antoinette (Annie) is indeed Boldness with a capital "B." Know also that your friend Donna is correct. As you grow into the essence of your angel, who was so carefully chosen for you, you will grow into your highest potential. Do as Donna did; put the intention out there to grow into the essence of your angel, if that is what you desire to do. The Universe is ready to rush in and manifest what it is you desire.

So, my dear, move onward and upward. We love you so deeply and support you in all that you do. Please ask what you will. We are here for you.

All our love,

The Angelic Realm

October 4, 2003

Dear Donna,

It is with great pleasure and anticipation that I make this contact with you. Yes, I will come to your aid whenever you call. Marc understands that my essence, my insightfulness, can be very helpful to one such as you, who has such an inquisitive mind. Please do not hesitate to ask. I will delight in solving puzzles for you that, if you were to try to solve on your own, might take "forever," or at least a great deal of your time and energy.

So, you are very happy with Henry and his work. Do not doubt for one millisecond that this encounter was planned. It has been in the making for a long time. Yes, you are indeed on a fast forward healing program, and Henry can help you with that process of becoming whole and well.

Henry has a very inquisitive mind as well. Now that he knows my name and my essence, we will become fast acquaintances. There is so very much we can do in the healing profession together. Henry knows the importance of asking. There is nothing left for us to do but "get the show on the road."

I love him so very, very much. Yes, I do tend to be quite intellectual, as you know. But, as you also know, I am very deeply caring and concerned…about Henry and all those who come to him for help. There are so many who do not know where to turn, who are lost, afraid and in pain. I truly want to reach out to all of them and to be a balm for them. Yes, I am insightful; this is true. But my deepest desire is to use my insightfulness to be a healing balm in the lives of humans, whom I love so very deeply.

Do not cry, my dear. The human race has only begun to understand this great love we feel toward it. But we are coming en masse, en masse. The time will come when the veil will be lifted and we will live in peace and harmony and love for one another.

Go now. You have another letter to write. Thank you for representing us so very well and for your love toward your fellow humans and us. You and I will be in touch. We have much in common.

Love,

Germaine

October 4, 2003

Dear Donna,

So, you get to type a letter for your beloved teacher, Sarah. If you had had your way, this would have been your first letter. But you have been obedient, and you have been very much following the guidance of Spirit. Good for you!

Please let me say a word about you first, my dear, and then we'll talk about Sarah. It is important that you, Donna, learn to be generous with yourself. This has recently been brought to your attention, but you are failing to heed the advice fully. It is imperative that each and every day you take the time to give yourself credit for that which has already been accomplished. You are always ready for "whatever is next," be it a letter, a phone call, or to send a note to someone to let that person know you appreciate his or her thoughtfulness. What the entire angelic realm and I wish to repeat to you over and over until you get it is that you must be as generous with kudos to yourself as you are to your students and those with whom you come into contact.

Now, let's talk about Sarah. Yes, I love Sarah very, very much. It is my true delight to be her angel. Generosity is her middle name, although one might have to look with magic glasses to see this. She has such a generous heart. She **allows** others to be who they are, to be where they are, and to just be okay with what is…at least for the time being. This is a fantastic concept. You Americans are so quick—quick to make judgments, quick to accept change (even for the worse), quick to cook your food. Quick! Quick! Quick! But doesn't it take someone with a heart overflowing with generosity to say: "I have so much, so very much. I want to give to you what I have. I have everything and I want to give everything to you. The best way that I can give to you everything that is yours to have is to allow you to be who you are." Yes, Sarah allows others to emerge into who they are, whoever that may be. She also trusts that whoever they are is good. It is her generosity of heart and her loving spirit that allows her to be the fantastic teacher that she is. I do not use this work "fantastic" lightly. I use it with the sincerest of hearts.

Donna, go, my child; you have done your work. Do not think any more this weekend about "what is next." Instead, take a look at your day and give yourself credit for a job well done. You will be guided in due time. We guide you to rest and to relax. Be generous with yourself in this area—please. We love you. We love Sarah.

Anita

October 13, 2003

Dear Donna,

Isn't it marvelous how spirit works? Almost with no effort at all, here you are, you and JoAnn, talking about love, speaking in tongues, angels and miracles. So much of life is a miracle, and yet so many people miss it! But the time is at hand for all to see the miracles that love can bring to their lives.

So, you are getting a little more comfortable with your gift. Hurray for you! Yes, we did have you on our shoulders today! Yes, Michael, your beloved friend and mighty archangel, brought you to us, if only for a few minutes, so that we could applaud you and tell you how much we love you. And, oh, how we do!

Yes, my essence is vivaciousness. And isn't my so, so sweet JoAnn full of vivaciousness? Why, it exudes from her every pore. It is like the sweet aroma of love that fills a room. It is like a garden in spring, exploding with color and life. It is like an autumn day in Indian summer. Oh, how it is my delight to be her angel and to see her move about her day, bringing joy and life to those with whom she talks and laughs. Oh, we have known each other for a long time. I am right by her ear. She hears me, but she just doesn't know it is I talking to her. But—oh—now she will know that it is I, Lizzy, who is whispering sweet nothings into her lovely ears! Yes, my "full" name is Louise, and JoAnn may call me that if she so desires. But my preference, if she is comfortable with it, is Lizzy. Lizzy has a little "zing" to it. Lizzy is full of life, as is my beloved human.

You know that we angels love our humans very much. More and more are feeling this love and being open to our influence in their lives. It is most important that you constantly remind people of their gift of free will. This is why it is so important that we be **asked** for help, guidance, direction, comfort, and so on. We need the "go ahead." How often we sit on the sidelines waiting, waiting, waiting to be asked. Our deepest longing is to be of service. We want to bridge the gap between heaven and earth. This is what we are all about! **But we must be asked!** Oh, how we long to rush in to do that which has been requested of us.

This is all for now. I do have a tendency to talk, I know. It is part of my vivaciousness. I know you don't mind. Some of us are real talkers, some are quieter, and some hardly talk at all, like Annabelle. But there are all kinds in the angelic realm, just as there are in your world.

This has been really great! Thank you so much—from the bottom of my heart. I am so excited that JoAnn knows my name and that we can become even better friends. You're the best!

Love,

Lizzy

Donna Allen

October 13, 2003

Dear Donna,

You and Barbara* have both known for some time that your friendship was not coincidental. And it is not. We will be asking Barbara to proofread your book, and she will be more than happy to do this for you.

We ask you to let go of the last bit of fear you are holding onto, so that your letters may flow swiftly onto your computer keys. It is our desire that you "work" with the greatest of ease and joy—which brings me to a subject dear to my heart.

My essence is joy. There is a wellspring of joy deep within Barbara that permeates her very being and expresses itself in so many ways. Her deep love for her four boys, her husband, her students and, hopefully, herself is what gives her life meaning and joy. May the joy that is within her come to full fruition. She is learning to trust herself more. She will be growing very quickly now that she knows my name. If only I can somehow convince her of this deep love that I have for her. She has so many fine gifts. It is my deepest hope that she will come to see them more clearly. She is such a devoted child of God; and her faith is much, much deeper than she realizes.

There seems little I can do at the moment to ease her discomfort over her job situation. But this communication is timely in that I can tell her that there is a definite purpose for it, one which she will understand in due time. Please let this letter serve as a reminder to her that she must ask for my intervention. I will run, and I do mean run, to carry out any task that she asks of me. My greatest joy is to be of service to Barbara. My most sincere wish is for her to see herself as I do. There is so much love, so much goodness, and a longing to be of service to others.

The heavens bless this friendship. It truly is in its beginning stages. We love you both and wish the best for you.

Cleo and the Angelic Realm

Barbara's response to her letter:

I am thankful for having met Donna for so many reasons. She has influenced my life in countless ways, and I am grateful for her friendship and support. But, most of all, she has put me in touch with my angel, Cleo, to whom I have prayed since I learned the "Angel of God" prayer in first grade. I have uttered this prayer thousands of times without knowing that God has created one angel just for me.

Now prayers to my angel have taken on another dimension as I call on Cleo by name and know that she is there for me. Knowing I have a special guardian angel has filled me with a sense of wonder and awe, and has shown me God's great love for me.

I thank God each day for the many blessings that He has showered upon me, and for Cleo, one of His greatest blessings.

Several letters in this book reference me doing healing work with others. I studied with Dr. Eric Pearl, and am certified to do Reconnective Healing™ sessions. I am also a Karuna Reiki® Master. Depending on the situation and the preferences of the individual, one of these healing modalities is used during our time together. The message of the following letter is intended for Jamie and me. Jamie's angel, Julia, was present during a healing session for my friend, Judy, which took place earlier in the day. Thus, there is a reference to me working on Judy.

October 16, 2003

Dear Donna,

I am so very glad you felt my presence so strongly as you worked on Judy this morning. You heard my name, felt my presence and acted upon my words. I will always be available to help you with your healing sessions and in all areas of your life. My essence is so tender, so sweet, and so delicious. It is so desperately needed by your world. Each time you work on someone, my essence will infiltrate his or her being and help to make your world a more tender and sane place to live and love.

Yes, I am Julia, beloved angel of Jamie. It is my longing to express my essence of tenderness through so many. And, yet, it is through Jamie that I can express myself most fully. Deep within her is this desire to be a balm of tenderness and compassion to all who come to her. She is delicately balancing all facets of her life—her personal life with family and friends, her patients, her students, and herself. She has a deep appreciation for the complexities of life and is in tune with the shifts that life can deal. She moves gently through her day, always aware of how she can be of help, how she can offer professional advice, how she can offer comfort and love. Oh my, what a joy it is to be her angel.

Thank you so much for following your promptings to go to her, for allowing yourself to be vulnerable so that you two could make the deep connection that you did. This relationship will continue. It will grow and many will benefit. There is so much good in the allopathic health community. There is so much good in the alternative health community. There will be a merging of these two worlds and people will be becoming whole and strong again. How much better it would be if people were as open to both worlds of good as you are.

So, my child, we will be in touch. You already see how your life has changed, even in this one day, by the greater awareness of tenderness brought to you by Jaime and me. Please send out the word: Tenderness is vital to our existence. It gives life meaning. It gives life joy.

As with all the other angels who have spoken with you in this rather formal manner of letter writing, I admonish you to tell my sweet Jamie that it is vitally important that she ask me for whatever it is she desires. I am here to serve her. Her will is free. She must ask. Oh, then I can rush in with all my talents and the talents and gifts of other angels to bless her and those for whom she cares so much.

You are becoming much more confident with your new gift. Soon the newness will wear off, and with it, the last bit of nervousness. Rushing in to fill the void will be the strength, courage, and power of your beloved Michael and

your tender, healing companion, Raphael. Go swiftly now.
I hold you in my angelic heart.

Love, peace, and tenderness

Julia

Down-to-Earth Angels

The following two letters are written for George (nickname for Georgianna) and Tari, two delightful women who co-own the beauty salon, G. T. Styling. I particularly enjoyed Cupid's pun "by George!"

October 16, 2003

Dear Donna,

I am just so excited! I get to talk to my George. Isn't she the greatest? She is so much fun, isn't she? She laughs when most people would cry. She makes others laugh and feel so comfortable. With her they can be themselves as with no one else.

However, I feel we need to talk about another matter for the moment. George works entirely too hard. The most difficult thing is that she doesn't see an alternative. But there is one, one she can't see at this time, but one that will be revealed to her in just a little while. I wanted her to know that this opportunity to not work quite so hard is coming so that she will be open to it. She has worked so hard for so long that she thinks that this is the way things have to be. But this is not true. Now that she has this information, she will be on the lookout for an alternative, which will serve her well.

Now that I have that said (and feel so much better for having said it), let's talk about my essence. My essence, as you already told George, is laughter. Laughter is the best medicine. It is akin to joy, and joy is what feeds the soul. Every time that one feels joy, one helps to make the world a better place. That joy that is felt radiates outward, affecting those within a very wide radius. So, it is joy, joy, joy that feeds the souls of your world. We live in our angelic world where there is so much joy that we are used to the feeling. You in your world are afraid of joy. You don't think you deserve it. **But you do!** You are the delightful creation of the Father and were created to live in peace, happiness, and joy!

So, my dear, sweet George, please, oh please, keep on laughing. You have no idea how many hearts you make lighter by your presence, your being, and your goodness. We in the angelic realm love you so very much. We long to serve you. Please say my name often. Even if you do not know what to ask for, please just say my name—Pumpernickle—and I will rush to your side and make my presence known to you.

Donna, thank you for letting me talk so much. You are truly patient and let us have our way as you sit down to type. We are all so eager to talk to our humans. As you have sensed, we are standing in line, hoping our turn will be next. But keep following your guidance. We will wait as long as need be. But we are indeed longing. Know we love you with all of our hearts.

Peace, joy, and laughter,

Pumpernickle

October 16, 2003

Dear Donna,

You sense my essence as you begin to type. You sense an ease, a naturalness that is not your own. You sense a calm, a gentleness, a longing even to be outside and one with nature. Yes, I am Cupid, Tari's angel, and my essence is naturalness.

The reason it took you awhile to "pick up" on my essence in the salon today, as you looked at Tari and wondered, is because for so long you have tried to be what you thought other people wanted you to be. As a child, young adult, and mature adult, you were not told to **be who you are**—which is love! This message did not come to you until recently, and you are only now becoming more comfortable with your true self.

Oh, but my sweet Tari is not a people pleaser. I love that about her. She is who she is. She is truly a "natural woman." And I love her so very much. That is why I chose the name Cupid, because my heart is attached to hers with an arrow that shoots through and through.

I wish to move on to my next subject. Tari misses her mother. Yet, her mother is as close as her very breath. If only somehow I could let her know that her dear, sweet mother is longing to ease her heavy heart and to let her know how very near she is. I think this letter will make her heart a little lighter. She will know that we are all close together. Those who pass on can communicate to their loved ones through us. We are a bridge between worlds, and our purpose and desire is to bring joy, peace and happiness to our humans.

So, my word to you is, first of all, thank you for letting me be next in line. (Actually, it is the Father who chooses, which you know!) But next, know there is a little room for improvement on your part in this area. Ah! You've asked for help! Yes, I can help you be your natural self; indeed, I can and I will, by George! (Pun intended!)

So, go now, faithful one. You have done your work well. Sleep well and let us minister to you as you lay your head upon your pillow.

Sweetest of dreams,

Cupid

November 10, 2003

Dear Donna,

We are so very happy that you are excited about writing again. May you feel all the joy that is to be had with your gift. It was necessary for you to wait a while. This will be explained to you at a later date. It is our intention for you to have your wish of typing letters for all of your Spirit Seed Sisters before the appointed date. However, we do want you to realize that at times you will be giving a person only their angel's name and their angel's essence. This is something that can be done on the spot, in a matter of seconds, and will have lasting effects.

You have known for weeks now that Diana's angel's name is Sweet Pea and that her angel's essence is cheerfulness. Think about Diana's smile and the sweet scent of cheerfulness that comes from her heart as she looks at you. It is warm and inviting. It says, "I am here. You are here. And this is good. Let us be who we are and get to know one another." Diana is indeed a nature babe. She is dedicated to the earth and to all that belongs to it. We on this side of the veil do all that we can to support those who love the earth and all that is in it. Earth is your home. Heaven is our home. These two worlds are becoming one because of people like Diana, people like you. We love all of you so very much. We do not have to deal with the struggles that you do, as we live on a different plane. We have so much hope, so much love, that it is sometimes difficult to appreciate what it is like to live in your world. But we tell you now and forever, **Be of good cheer. Be Cheerful and Rejoice!** A new day is dawning, one in which all men, women, children, and all the living things on the face of the earth will say—Life is Good! Let us live in peace and harmony with one another.

The Harmonic Concordance has ushered in a new age. Change will be taking place so fast that "heads will be spinning." But hang on for the ride, for it will be a glorious one. There is no time to waste. Love **must** dwell in the hearts of humankind for it to survive. Can a fish live without water? Can the birds fly without air? Can humankind live without love? You get the point.

Diana, please keep being the cheerful person that you are. So gentle. So kind. So good. We love you and all you hold dear, including your beloved child. Go forward unafraid of being who you are. We need you. Your world needs you.

So much love to you and yours,

Sweet Pea and the Angelic Realm

Diana's response:

I am so grateful for my angel letter. Conscious awareness of Sweet Pea has made my life sweeter! Talking with Sweet Pea makes my heart warm!

Down-to-Earth Angels

November 11, 2003

Dear Donna,

It is with **great** anticipation that I write to you and to my beloved Judy. She is the apple of my eye, my true delight. I love her so very much, and now I have a chance to tell her just that, to put it in writing.

Yes, my essence is energy and my name is Jack. I just **know** that Judy is going to like my name. Actually, she is quite easy to please. She has had it difficult, but one would never know it at first glance. She is just so full of life, so full of love, so full of joy. Why, one can hardly talk to her for even one minute without being uplifted. She uses her energy for such good, to help so many people. She is just a sweet, sweet person. How could anyone help but love her?

Let me talk to you, Donna, for just a moment about energy. You have suffered from "low energy" for most of your life. Do you know why? It is because you were trying to be something you are not—less than love. This has been addressed before with you, but it bears repeating. Your essence is love. You **must** be the love that is you. When you are who you are, energy will abound. Right now you are still finding your place in the grand scheme of things, but soon all of that will be made clear…and then, wow! Look out world! In the meantime, get all the rest you need, because much work is done on you at night, as you already know. Back to Judy….

There is so much I could say to my Judy. But what I wish to say most of all to her is…Judy, I love you so very much. I have been with you since the time you were born and will be with you until you take your last breath. Please call upon me when you have need of **anything**, just **anything**. I will come running. I would love you to **consciously** run with me, swim with me, talk with me, and be with me. For you to be conscious of my presence would bring me such joy that I could scarce take it in.

This is all for now. Please find joy in our relationship. I truly long for that. I do.

I love you so.

Jack

Judy's response:

I would be honored to have my letter included in your book.

November 13, 2003

Dear Donna,

We sense a tinge of nervousness as you begin to type. We also sense a deep respect on your part for your work and your role in mediating between our worlds. We thank you for that reverence and for the regard you give to doing your job for us well.

We love you; this you know now well. You are becoming more and more confident in your gift and in your guidance. Things will be progressing very rapidly now. You want to know how you can follow guidance more easily, how you can ease the pain in your stomach. Ask for all doubt to be removed. Ask for greater faith. These will be given to you in increasing measure.

My Cindy is very anxious, even longing, to know my name. She will be very pleased to know that I am, indeed, a male angel and that my name is Ethan. I am very strong, as is she. I am very genuine, as is she. My essence is genuineness. I long to express myself through humankind and am indeed reaching so many, many more with each passing day. It is through my Cindy that I can and do express my essence very, very fully.

What do we mean by genuineness? When one is genuine, one expresses one's thoughts, feelings, and ideas in a very clear, understandable manner that is not offensive to others. It is a very valuable trait and one that allows for meaningful human interaction. If one says, "Oh, s/he is such a genuine person," the other automatically feels a sense of deep trust toward that person. Yes, trusting a genuine person is a very easy thing to do.

We in the angelic realm know there is an awful lot of distrust upon planet Earth. This must not continue. Humans must learn to trust themselves and each other and to be genuine in their concern for one another. Many are already doing this. But many others, way too many others, are very far away from where they need to be in this area.

Those of you who are bringing more and more light to planet Earth are the ones who are also bringing a sense of genuineness to your world. Please, all of you, think about the ways you relate to one another. Let there be no little white lies. Let there be no small acts of unkindness. Each person can and does make a **huge** difference. We implore you to be kind and tenderhearted in your interactions with one another. Please, oh please, be genuine.

My dear Cindy, I love you so very much. You know my name. Please call on me often. You are so good, so sweet, and so kind; all these attributes go hand in hand with genuineness. It is my pleasure to by your angel. Please, oh please, let's be the best of friends.

So much love for you in my heart,

Ethan

Cindy's response:

Dear Donna,

Thank you for "signing up" to be a conduit through which our angels can contact us. I am sure you are an incarnated angel who has volunteered to assist us from this side, and what valuable work it is!

What a thrill to be contacted by my angel, Ethan, in your letter. I was deeply moved to be described as genuine and strong and to be told that my essence is appreciated and needed in the world today. How life affirming! For so long, I have wanted to have knowledge of my angel or spirit guide. To now have a name to call upon is so wonderful. I will definitely use it often and build a relationship with Ethan. We will be the best of friends, for sure.

Thank you again, Donna, for fulfilling the longing in many of us to know that we are not alone and that we have a connection to the other side that helps to sustain us in our times of struggle and uncertainty in the world today.

Sincere blessings for your continued success as your writing progresses and your book is complete.

Cindy

November 15, 2003

Dear Donna,

It surprises us that you would be a little nervous about writing about an angel whose essence is "cuteness." What would the world be like without cute this and that? Oh my, how boring it would be. Think about little girls with turned-up noses. Think about puppy dogs and kittens and all of the other little babes in the animal kingdom. Webster says that to be cute is to be pretty or attractive, especially in a lively, wholesome, or dainty way. Doesn't your world need beauty, attractiveness, liveliness, and daintiness? Do not underestimate the **great power** in cuteness. Whatever uplifts the human soul is powerful.

That is why my Candi is so powerful. Her essence, like mine, is cuteness. She is not only powerful, she is bold in her love—very much like your sweet Deirdre. She does not hesitate to reach out to others with her love, her power, and her cuteness. Perhaps it is time for you and others to broaden your appreciation of this word and its meaning.

There is more we could say about cuteness, but you seemed a little blocked. Perhaps instead we can talk a little about what happened at the prayer meeting, if you are open to that. Candi was sharing with the group—about Justin and his older sister as well as her own son. She was sharing her concern and their sense of loss. In love you reached out to her and touched her. You felt her energy say: "Please don't touch me just now. I need your love but I also need space to feel and to express what it is I am feeling." There is a time to touch and there is a time to listen in love without rushing in to comfort. As you learned at the Sophia Center, through your beloved teacher Sarah, there is an art to listening. Often, one rushes in to comfort when allowing space is the more appropriate and more loving thing to do. Do not be hard on yourself for touching when you should have allowed for space. You are learning.

Candi, please know that I am so very happy to be your angel. I am very proud of my essence and am very happy to express that essence through you. Please say my name often. I am already in your heart, as you know, and long to be the best of friends. You are always on mind, and I am anxious for us to work together, spreading love, good cheer, and many kindnesses to others. Please ask Donna any questions you might have.

So much love and sweetest of blessings,

Angelina

Candi's response:

Dear Donna,

I'm sorry it has taken so long for my response. I have company coming and going and a flooded basement. I didn't want to rush my response because I believe this to be important work.

For me the importance lies in the fact that I really never gave much thought to angels as individual essences. Not that I didn't believe, I just never put thought into it. I have felt alone most of my life and yet not alone. I knew there was spirit within and without, yet I didn't know how to further tap into it.

Over the last four to five years, I have been learning to do just that. I still, however, feel I am still in kindergarten. We humans seem to make life much more difficult than it needs to be.

Hearing an angel with a name speak directly of me and to me was such a joy. I am so grateful. I do speak to her and say her name often—Angelina. When I do, I always feel comforted and know she wants to extend to me her love. It has added another beautiful and welcomed dimension to my spiritual path. So I remain grateful for your dialogues with angels, and I am sure whoever reads them will feel the same. I look forward to reading them all. I send this with much love, Candi

December 1, 2003

Dear Donna,

It has been some time since you have written, hasn't it? It was necessary for you to learn that you don't need to feel that tremendous surge of inspiration to sit and to type. You have always been "good at doing your homework." It takes discipline and time and willingness. So, too, typing angel letters, books, responding to people's questions, etc. takes these same qualities. You no longer need to wait for the urging of us angels. Please just do your work in a relaxed and comfortable manner.

You have had some concern about typing angel letters, as you call them, for your Spirit Seed sisters. You will complete this task and it will be a joyous one for all involved. We were a little concerned, as we expressed to you in the past, that you would not make it to the Spirit Seed Institute. We were also concerned that you might not return for the second segment. We know it was difficult for you and for all the Spirit Seed sisters. Spiritual growth can sometimes be so very challenging, as you well know. Oh, but to hear the Master's voice, to feel the peace and love of Mary, and to come to know your guides, teachers, and angels, whoever they may be and from whatever spiritual tradition they might come! Rejoice! It is time for world renewal!

It is our wish at this time to address Carol. Carol, the essence of your angel is loyalty. You epitomize this quality. Your loyalty to your beloved daughter is unquestionable. We applaud you in this. We want you to know that both you and your daughter have many angels who surround you day and night, watching, loving, encouraging. Please ask any and all of us what we can do to help. Please include in your prayers that you would like to grow into the essence of your angel, Princess Diana. You may call your angel Diana if you are more comfortable with that, or you may call her Princess. It is your choice. We all love you so very much and cannot tell you that strongly enough. Your love of dolls is a true gift. Continue to share that love.

Behold, the time is at hand for all humans to come to intimately know their angels. You can and will help tremendously in this process. You will be guided.

So much love to you and yours,

Princess Diana and the Angelic Realm

As I mentioned previously, for the first few months after I started writing angel letters, all of the letters were addressed to me but contained information about another person. I truly longed to take more of a back seat, and for the letters to be addressed to the person for whom the message was intended. Thus, I was extremely delighted when the following letter began "Dear Kathleen…" I did realize that this probably occurred because it was the second letter I was writing that day; the angels had already spoken to me in the previous letter, and they evidently didn't feel they needed to say any more.

December 1, 2003

Dear Kathleen,

I am just so very excited about being able to write to you. I hope you don't mind that I have chosen the name "Giggles." It was just something I **had** to do. You know what I mean. That is my essence too! I just love to giggle! You know, whenever I start to giggle, all my angel friends just join in. Before you know it, we're all sitting around just giggling our silly heads off. And when **you** giggle… well, I just giggle all the more. So, maybe you will be open to **consciously** giggling with me. I just love it when I hear some authoritative human say to some sweet children…now girls, stop your giggling. Why, such a silly thing to say. Giggling is just so much fun. And when the girls can't and won't stop giggling…well that just warms my little ole heart to the core.

What many humans don't understand is that the soul **needs** to giggle. It brings about such a lightness of being that every cell in the body is revitalized and made more whole. So, what I say is—giggle to your heart's content and you will be the wiser and the healthier for it. Giggle. Giggle. Giggle. Have I got you doing it yet?

There is so much inside of you that wants to express itself. You do not have to be or do anything that you are not already being or doing. But your being longs to express itself through verse, and that longing is leading you in the direction you are going. There are so many books that you need to write. So many stories that you need to tell. And believe you me, there is a huge listening audience who needs to hear what you have to tell. So, Kathleen, please tell your stories. Please keep up your laughing, and your giggling.

I love you so very much and cannot wait to express myself more fully through you, through your writings and through your encounters with others. You will grow into my essence and into a genuine expression of who you are. Please say my name often. We **will** be in touch.

With heartfelt thanks for being your angel,

Giggles

Kathleen's response:

Dear Donna,

When I first read that my angel's name was Giggles, I couldn't believe it. Giggles? What kind of a name is that for an angel? It sounded very childish. But as I read the letter, I realized that Giggles was perfect for me. It is childlike rather than childish, and it celebrates the lightheartedness of me. As I read through it, I did start to giggle, and those listening to me read the letter aloud did too.

Of course, we should giggle and laugh and guffaw as often as possible. It is so uplifting to Spirit, mine as well as those around me.

The part of the letter where Giggles talked about all the things I have to say and all the books in me literally screamed out at me. Yes! Yes! Yes! I am in the process of writing three books right now, and I have ideas for several others. I also am working on several speeches and have lots and lots of stories to tell. So it feels as if my angel knows me very well. I have been praying to her every day, so that we can join together as quickly as possible to get my thoughts and ideas out into the world.

Thank you so much for introducing me to Giggles. I love her and love having her as a part of my life. I can't wait until we actually join as one. Look out world, here we come!

Love, Kathleen

December 2, 2003

Dear Donna,

You still marvel at your gift, and we see this as a good thing. But you have many gifts that are just part of you that you don't necessarily marvel at anymore. You are very kind; yet, this is something that you had to work at. Kindness has become your hallmark, yet at one time you did not take it for granted. So, too, it will be with your gift. You will be able to sit at a typewriter with people hanging over your shoulder; and with no discomfort at all, you will type a letter for them. You have sensed this coming. We know that you would love to be able to see us angels as does Louise Cook and Mary Ellen. We wish to stay mute on this point at this time. But as Marc told you over a year and a half ago, put it out there. There will be a time when we angels will be quite visible to many, many humans, not just a few. Rejoice! We are coming en masse!

May I please speak to my dear Kathleen? Oh, how my sweetheart is so full of trust. Yes, that is my essence—trust. You, Donna, are growing in trust every single day. Kathleen is so full of trust that it exudes from her every pore. Why, when she speaks, the quality of her voice says that she trusts in God, in good, in life, and in the goodness of all that is. This is why she is so full of joy. She has so very little doubt in her. She goes on her merry way, knowing that all that she needs will come to her. I rejoice in her trust. I feel so very close to her because my essence permeates her being. She has much to share with the rest of the world on how she came to be such a trusting person. I would like to ask her to consider at this time how she might do that. It can be done in a wide variety of ways, and I will be more than happy to help her with that "project."

Kathleen, I have been waiting so very patiently for my turn to write. We angels love you humans so very much. Please ask me for help with whatever it is you would like; yet, you know that trust is a prayer in and of itself. So often, the Lord whispers "trust me." Sometimes those words are heeded and a blanket of peace overcomes the receiver. Sometimes the question becomes: "How can I trust you?" Then the anxiety continues, sometimes endlessly.

The time has come when trust must have its day. Humans cannot live happily without a deep and abiding trust in the Divine, however they understand the Divine. So, again I ask you to teach the world, your own world, about trust. Trust is your highest potential. Trust is who you are.

Be still, my heart. I have spoken to my beloved. Kathleen, call upon me. Say my name often. I could never tire of serving you and of loving you. All for now.

Your devoted angel,

Simon

Kathleen's response:

Trust was and is a perfect message for me, and yet it surprised me. At the time I received my angel Simon's letter, I would have appeared to be a very trusting person. To a certain degree, I was. However, my trust had limits attached to it. I would extend it only so far and then check to make sure all was going well according to my definitions and perspective.

Yet, trust isn't about definitions and limits or my perspective, which is much too confining. Trust is full and deep belief, and that level of belief comes only from love. For if one truly loves, "Love bears all things, believes all things, hopes all things, endures all things. Love never fails..." (Corinthians 13). This is trust; I do believe this, though I'm certainly not there yet!

May this angel's letter speak to you, too, and call to your heart. May it encourage you. May it perhaps allow you to be willing to take a risk (small or big) because you just don't want to feel this way anymore or because you are ready for something new to begin. Trust. The name Simon in Hebrew means "God listens." Believe all things are possible.

December 2, 2003

Dear Donna,

We find it amusing that you can "pick up on" us squabbling over whose turn it is to write. We are glad you laughed and were not judgmental of us. We angels do have our squabbles, as do all of you. I know I tend to want to get my own way, and I am a little bit "pushy," you might say, if I need to be.

My essence is sweetness; and my dear, dear Kristin is the sweetest of the sweet. (She likes to get her own way, too, I'm very happy to say!) There is so very much we could say about sweetness. Think of all of the sugar that you put into your foods and beverages! (This, by the way, is not healthy at all and is causing a host of health problems. So unnecessary!) No, the real sweetness of life is not something that can be appreciated with the taste buds. It is a feeling, a lightness, an appreciation for all that is good about life itself. It is the joy of a newborn babe. It is the sweet rising of the sun, as well as the setting of the sun. It is a cool glass of clean water to quench the thirst. It is the look of devotion in the eyes of a lover.

So much of the joy and sweetness of life is lost in all the hurrying and scurrying to gain fame and fortune. Oh, the need to simplify is so very great. Please, humans, simplify your lives. There is great meaning in the simplified life. One who lives a simple life knows what is important, what really counts. The media has programmed all of you into thinking that you are not good enough, not worthy enough. So you all go out and try to buy what will make you feel okay, sexy, and loved. Oh, but this is not the path to happiness or fulfillment. You are worthy. You are loved. Not because you buy this or that product, but because you are a creation of the Divine, who does not **ever** make a mistake.

I suppose all of this could seem like a digression, but I assure you it is not. Less **is** more. To taste the real sweetness of life, priorities must be in order. A conscientious effort must be made to prioritize one's life and to live according to one's values and beliefs. Otherwise, the influence of the media can overcome and so much is lost. So, hail to sweetness! May all of humanity taste the real sweetness that life has to offer.

Kristin, you are the sweetest person in the world! (I'm your angel, so I can say that.) I am with you all the time, and I witness daily how you sweeten the lives of your loved ones and those with whom you come into contact. You, my dear, have your priorities straight! As a side note, I'm happy you made it comfortably down the aisle this last time. You did beautifully! You are beautiful! You are sweet! You are my love.

Tinkerbell

Kristin's response:

Dear Donna,

I think it is wonderful that you are moving forward with *Down-to-Earth Angels*, as I know how pure your intentions are to encourage others to allow themselves to be open to the love that surrounds them, in this case by angels. I don't think I could add anything to what my angel says that would enhance the message. I know that I frequently struggle with keeping my priorities in line, and not being distracted by the "hurrying and scurrying to gain fame and fortune." But when I allow myself to slow down, it becomes possible (not automatic, but *possible*) to appreciate what "is good about life itself." So I will join with my angel in the wish and blessing: "May all of humanity taste the real sweetness that life has to offer."

I wish you, Donna, all the peace and happiness that you so richly deserve, and I hope your readers are able to absorb the love and beautiful messages the angels and you wish to impart.

Hail to sweetness, Kristin

December 7, 2003

Dear Donna,

Do not let the troubles you are having with your computer throw you from typing this letter. Perhaps you will have to call for some expert help.

We are very glad that you were not thrown off course when Martha told you that Louise Cook told her that her primary angel is Marcela. There is so much truth out there. Doreen Virtue tells her people that each person has two primary angels. You are telling people that they have one. So many books have been written about angels, although you have primarily read only what Doreen has had to say. What we wish to tell you is that no one individual has a monopoly on the truth.

We could say that truth is a relative thing, and that would be a true statement. But what we wish to emphasize more than anything is the power of speaking one's truth and living in one's truth. As one grows, his or her truth becomes more full, more encompassing, and more empowering. The truth of yourself that you are experiencing today is a different, an expanded truth from the truth of who you were a year ago, a decade ago. Truth is always evolving, ever changing.

What we wish to emphasize to you, Donna, is that we wish you to proclaim truth as you understand it today. Do not worry about what others will think, not ever. To do so will prevent you from expressing who you are and what you believe; it will thwart you in doing your work. Go proudly in your work. Will there be critics? Of course there will be. Remember what Linda Schaefer said at her presentation a couple weeks ago: Mother Theresa had her critics! Do what you know to be true for **you** through your own experience. Who you are and what you have experienced will be very valuable to many others. Many speak when they have little to say. Others do not speak because they do not have the whole truth, nothing but the truth, so help them God. Yet, no one can know the whole truth, because the whole truth has not been revealed! So, rejoice, your time is at hand. Be free at last from what you heard too often as you were growing up: "What will people think?" People will think what they will think. You should not speak based upon what you think they might want to hear. **Speak your truth**. Henry and you have talked briefly upon this. Now is the time for action.

Yes, this letter is for Deborah*, and she will be very tolerant that so much of it has been addressed to you. It was necessary. Deborah, my dear, sweet Deborah, is learning this valuable lesson of speaking and living her truth. She is becoming very adept at this, I am pleased to say. My name is Hardy. By my nature I am courageous and bold. I speak my truth with a tone of assurance that what I am saying is true for **me**. Other angels have their own truth and speak their truth according to their own levels of growth. We are **all growing, all evolving**.

Do not be concerned that Deborah will be disappointed with this letter. Yes, most of it was addressed to you and to the world, but it will hold deep meaning for her and she will understand. Deborah, know that I love you very much. We are one. Our friendship will grow, as will your

Donna Allen

ability to speak and live your truth. I am grateful that I am your angel.

With a heart full of love, courage, and honesty,

Your devoted angel, Hardy

December 3, 2003

Dear Donna,

Yes, take a deep breath. There are a few of us who wish to address you, and this is new for you. We wish to let you know that you **are** worthy and that we wish to address you as an equal.

Donna, I am so very pleased that you have been open to me comforting you and your family with regards to Leah. Yes, for the sake of others, I will identify myself. I am Mary, the beloved mother of Jesus. Yes, I did hold Leah as you and your family members held her, and she has been in my constant care. You must know how much I love you. You must know how very grateful I am to you for your devotion to me and to my beloved son, Jesus. There is nothing either of us would not do for you. I am happy you love your rosary bracelet so much and that it brings you so much comfort. Please know I am always by your side, bringing you the love of a devoted mother and friend. Yes, this is all I wish to say at this time. I love you.

Donna, as Linda Schaefer said, I am a Mother of few words. I am a Mother of action. Yes, I did appear to you that night a while ago and remind you to send a gift to the family of Nelson and Francisco, your sponsored children in Guatemala. And yes, I did speak to you the other evening on your ride home from your parish. I do see the spiritual impoverishment in your country, which is indeed why I do not want children in my orphanages to be adopted by those of your country. But you did hear me correctly: Your mission is to feed the spiritually poor of your country. Oh, the impoverishment. Oh, the impoverishment. Know that God is with you, always. Know that I am with you, always. I love you, too, dear heart.

You feel this is too much and so you shed tears. And yet there is one more who would like to address you and that is I, Mary Ann's angel. My name is Mary, and my essence is devotion. Mary Ann has always been so devoted to those of the Christian tradition. It is difficult to know what to say about devotion because it is such a vast subject and can mean so many different things to different people. One can be devoted to family, friends, God, a career, a cause, or a mission. Devotion comes from the core of one's being, from a well deep within where all that one is finds expression. Devotion is so needed in your human culture. How does one cultivate devotion? It is a gift, in a way. But it also is a quality that can be nurtured and brought to fruition. Mary was devoted to Love. Mother Theresa was devoted to Love. And we all know that God is Love. So, however one conceives of God, of Love, is where one should put his or her attention to grow in devotion.

So, Mary Ann, I am your devoted angel. I come to you with a heart full of love and devotion. You are so very sweet and express your devotion to all those and all that you hold dear in myriad ways. I am so very proud of you. I am so very happy to be your angel. Please speak to me often. Let me whisper in your ear. Let me guide you. May your devotion grow exponentially, and may you share your secrets of devotion to all those who have ears to hear. Share what you know about devotion with all who will listen. Devotion is oft underrated in your world. We would like it to be elevated to its rightful place in the universe. Hail to devotion! Hail to all that is good and holy!

We know this has been quite a serious letter. We also know the value of humor. So readers, take what you can of value from this letter and leave the rest for now. One must grow at his or her own pace. We do not wish to stress anyone or ask more than what one is ready for. We love all of you so very much.

With hearts full of love and devotion

Mary, Mother of Jesus

Mother Theresa

Mary, Mary Ann's Angel

Mary Ann's response to her letter:

My devotion to Mary is both my inspiration and my sanctuary. I believe that the Holy Mother of All, Mary, is an expression of my own blessed Divinity...the beautiful "face and heart" of the feminine face of God. I also am devoted to Mary because of her universal expression of "heart energy," being in an eternal state of unconditional love. In that place of unconditional love comes a wellspring of hope, trust, acceptance, patience, forgiveness, and compassion. These qualities embody the "holy" components that lead me to find sanctuary in her presence and guidance to live out the Divine Plan during my time on this good Earth.

December 14, 2003

Dear Donna,

You have asked that I not speak too long to you, that this letter is meant to be a Christmas present for Lynne, beloved daughter of Martha. I will honor that request.

My essence is adventurousness. By my very nature, I am strong and full of life. I love the unexpected. I love what is just around the corner, just a tad out of my sight. I long to experience life in its fullness. I am bold and daring. I am who I am and not afraid to be who I am.

My name is Huckleberry, and I am Lynne's angel. Lynne was born to one such as Martha, because she needed such a mother to be who she is, a lover of adventure. Martha has been willing to take risks herself; and thus, she has allowed her daughter to do the same. Martha, and now Lynne, understands that to be fully alive, one must be willing to risk. No, the safe and sure way is not the way of the adventurer.

Martha and Lynne will be traveling to India together shortly. And oh, what an adventure awaits them. To be in the energy of Sai Baba is something the two of them will take with them throughout their entire life journey. For a mother and daughter to take risks together is very powerful, very life transforming. They will be richly blessed, and others will be blessed by their daring and bold natures.

Lynne has many adventures in store. This is how she was destined to live her life. One adventure after another. She will never be bored. She will not settle for the mundane. She is courageous, though she might not see herself in that light. Often one does not see clearly who he or she is.

Flowers do not know their own beauty. Yet, I tell you that Lynne is indeed very beautiful and I rejoice in her adventurous nature.

May I speak to you for a moment, Donna? Marc has said to you more than once—Let it be an adventure. So often you want to know what the future holds. Yet the entire angelic realm and I would like you to adopt, if only a little bit, the adventuresome spirit of your friend Martha and her daughter Lynne. When one has the work to do that you have, an attitude of "joy in adventure" can and will do so very much to reduce the stress of the unknown. Please think and pray on this. Life is truly meant to be an adventure!

So, Lynne, know that I love adventure, too. I will be going to India with you. I will. For you to be conscious of my presence would bring me great joy. I will be with you whether you are conscious of me or not. But I would love to know that I am in your heart and that my name is on your lips. Please ask me for help whenever you need it. I am only a call away. I **will** come running to help. Someone who loves adventure as much as you can truly benefit from being aware of the power of her angel to come to her aid.

I so look forward to our friendship growing and growing. It will truly be an adventure for both of us. Please tell your mother that I am so very grateful to her. I am grateful that she has been courageous enough to let go of you. I am grateful that she asked Donna to write this letter.

I truly cannot tell you how much I love you. Donna feels this tremendous love and it has brought her to tears. That is as it should be. The love I feel for you is overpowering for me as well at times. I do love you so.

Donna Allen

I wish you and yours a Merry Christmas from the bottom of my heart.

With love beyond expression,

Huckleberry

Lynne's response:

One of the best things I got out of having this letter is my new constant traveling companion. Everywhere I go now I feel like I'm sharing the good and bad of an adventure with Huckleberry. Plus I feel like my desire to go off and do adventurous things is more justified. I wouldn't want to let Huckleberry down!

Down-to-Earth Angels

I was once again delighted when the following letter came addressed to the person for whom the message was intended—in this case, Christine*. I was assuming that it was possibly because it was the second letter I'd typed that day. However, I was also hopeful that perhaps the angels were finding I had gained enough confidence in my work that they did not need to speak to me in each letter, and thus did not need to address the letters to me. My hope was well founded. From this point forward, all the letters are addressed directly to the recipient!

December 14, 2003

Dear Christine*,

As Donna sits to type this letter for you, she takes a deep breath and trusts that all will happen according to plan. So, too, when you perform, you take a big breath and just go for it. There is trust involved in writing letters for those whom one has never met. There is a great deal of trust involved in getting on a stage in front of an audience and performing.

When one performs, no matter what form that performance might take, there is an element of risk involved. What if I make a mistake? What if people laugh? What if I fall flat on my face? Can this level of success be met again? Can I improve upon my current level of success?

Oh, but the joy of doing what one is called to do, to express what is in one's being. God, the Creator, deeply understands the need to express, to create, to allow that which is deep within to reach out and thrust itself upon the Universe. God delights in expression, creative expression, if you will.

I am your beloved angel, and I have taken on the name C. E. My name is Creative Expression. I know this is a very unusual name for an angel, but it suits me just fine, because that is my essence also. (Please note that your mom's angel has a two-initial name also. Perhaps that will make it easier for you to accept my name, which I really, really like.)

Creative Expression has become a buzzword these past few years, relatively speaking. As the basic needs of humankind are met, higher level needs can be felt and attended to. One of the highest needs of humans is to be the creative beings that they are. You, my dear, sweet Christine, find expression in the Performing Arts, and that delights me to no end. So often people wear masks. They find a little niche, get very comfortable, identify themselves according to that niche, and then stay there the rest of their lives. Even when they get very uncomfortable with the little hole they have created for themselves, they are afraid to say: "This is not working. I am not comfortable here anymore." So, they stay put. They stagnate. Then they die and wonder what their life was all about.

People are not meant to create niches for themselves. No, they are meant to be alive, creative, loving human beings. This life on earth is not play practice. It is the real thing. Life is meant for the living. It is meant for good. It is meant that humans grow into their Divine potential now, this time around.

Christine, I, your angel C. E., love all that you stand for. You stand for courage, because it takes courage to stand on a stage in full view of an audience. You stand for youth. The youth stand for hope for the future. You stand for life. You are willing to express what it is inside you that seeks expression, in all its myriad forms.

You, like your sister Lynne, were born to a dear, sweet mother who knew that her children would long to express themselves, even as she has longed to express herself. To try to stifle the innate nature of one's child does that child a huge disservice. This stifling did not happen to you or to Lynne. You have parents who want for you what it is you want. They knew that to try to put you into a box labeled "this is how my child should and must be" would be tantamount to killing your spirit, the essence of who you are.

So, my dear, you have been blessed. You have been given permission to be and to express who it is that you are. Oh, if only this permission would be given to all children upon the face of the earth. God gives his children this permission. But too often parents do not allow their children the space they need to breathe, to be a full, creative expression of their spirits.

Christine, please continue to give expression to the sweetness of your spirit. By your courage and your example, you give others permission to do the same. I love you so very much, perhaps even as much as your parents, although the love we all have for you should not be compared.

I have a favor to ask of you. Would you please take me onto the stage with you? I long to express who I am, too. I would love to be up in front of the audiences with you. Please consider this. Know that I am always with you, always. As you sleep. As you wake up in the morning. When you are with friends and family. As you memorize your lines. Always.

May you have the most blessed of Christmases. I love you deeply.

C. E.

PS, If you prefer to call me something different, that's okay with me. My essence will remain the same no matter what you choose to call me. Honest.

Christine's response:

Dear Donna,

What an amazing angel I have. Since reading the letter, I've become more aware of her presence. Perhaps it helps to put a name to a feeling. I've recently been playing with oracle cards by Doreen Virtue. In the faery set, there is a card called "Creative Expression." The faery on it is a bit ugly and the card is nothing special, but I feel it is a sort of direct contact with my C. E. Whenever I ask for random advice or guidance, I pull this card out of a very shuffled deck. This happens enough times to override coincidence. This has been such a comfort to me! I've reached a new part in my life, and the comfort I've gotten from the letter and the more intimate knowledge of my angel are invaluable. Thank you, Donna, for opening this up to me. Christine

December 22, 2003

Dear Amy,

It meant a lot to Donna that she was able to share with you and Pam that she is writing a book. This work means a great deal to her, and to know that she can share the depths of her being with long time friends is very comforting and supportive. She loves you and will be keeping you and your whole family in her prayers, as will I.

I am Jonathan, your angel. My essence is reverence. Reverence, a feeling of respect and awe for the sacred, has taken a back seat in your culture, as you well know. What only a short time ago was considered to be special, sacred, and worthy of reverence is now treated with a lackluster attitude at best. Often the best the world has to offer is scoffed at, ridiculed, made light of, or debased.

Everything that God has created is good. But humankind has in too many ways taken the joy out of that which was created to bring happiness and a sense of meaning and fulfillment to the human race. Of course, sex is at the top of this list. It has reached its lowest form in your culture. The media, affecting the minds of young and old alike, has made millions selling a wrong message. Sex was originally designed to bring great pleasure, to be an expression of deep love and, of course, to continue the human race. It is now sold as a commodity. People are using one another. Hearts are left empty, broken, and bitter. But sex is only one of God's gifts that are being so badly misused.

What the world needs now is so much more love. We angels express love at its fullest. God is love, and so are we. What people are **really** looking for is love. A healthy love of self. A deep sense of connection to their fellow humans. And a heartfelt sense of oneness with their higher power (I know, a Twelve Step term), whom some choose to call God. When some read these letters, they might think we sound "flaky" or "unreal." It is because we talk about love all the time. We cannot help but talk about that which we are.

We care so very deeply about all the little details of your daily lives because you care about them. Do not the cares of the beloved become the cares of the lover? Do not the concerns of the child become the concerns of the loving parent? Likewise, what matters to you matters to us. This is why when you ask for help, guidance, or protection, we immediately come to your aid. We want to express our love for you and actually look for ways to do that.

Amy, what I wish to express to you more than anything is my love for you. Donna has explained to you the importance of asking me for whatever it is you desire. She has explained that you have a free will and that I can in no way interfere with your free will, unless you are faced with a life-threatening situation and your time is not at hand. But what I want so very much is to be a big and important part of your life. Yes, this is my desire; and it is my hope that you will want us to be friends and partners. It can be a joyful relationship.

Please know that I have seen **all** of your struggles, and there have been many. I have been with you, offering love, support and comfort to you and those whom you love so very dearly. I see all the love you give your dear husband and your sweet, oh so sweet children. I see the deep reverence you have for all that is good, venerable and holy. I see the respect you command from your children and others because of your sense of respect for all that is worthy.

I take leave of you now. But know that I am **always** by your side. I walk with you. I respect you deeply. I love those whom you love. I am your constant friend and companion.

With love and respect,

Jonathan

Amy's response:

Dear Donna,

I don't know how to explain what a gift this is that you have given to so many others and me. I have read and reread this letter from my Jonathan so many times. When you first handed me the envelope, I tucked it away for a special time to be alone with its message. I find such continual comfort in its message and the fact that it came from you, a trusted friend. It is sincere and genuine in the purest form.

I was so anxious to see what the essence of my angel was. I now feel that I have been reawakened and made aware that, yes, *reverence* is really important to me. When I asked Pam what her essence was, I was so amazed that her essence, that one word, could describe her better than any list of qualities.

I had read the letter again just last week before we knew that Hurricane Charley was headed directly to Tampa Bay. We spent the day getting the house ready for the storm, and then left at six o'clock the next morning for the Fort Lauderdale area to my sister's home. As a northerner, I have always wondered what I would take with me if I were evacuated, and, of course, I had this long list. In reality, you really don't have much time or room; I took one photo of my kids that I know no one else has, and my dog. Out on the highway I kept thinking of my angel and wishing that this storm would just dissipate and that my home would be safe. Unlike our snowstorms that are most times never as bad as predicted or just fade away without much fanfare, hurricanes have to go somewhere. I felt so guilty that I was safe and that so many others lost so much. We passed several convoys of utility trucks and tree service companies on the road, and many gas stations with no gas left to pump. So whatever we are going through, it is always a comfort to know that my angel is always there.

I wish you all the success imaginable. You are really an inspiration to follow your dreams. Love, Amy

December 23, 2003

Dear Pam,

I would like to repeat to you what Amy's angel told Amy yesterday. Your being open to Donna and all that she had to tell you about her "story" was very comforting. You and Donna have known each other for many years. It would be easy to shy away from sharing such a life-changing event with old friends. The concern of rejection would be normal. Yet, you welcomed Donna and what she had to share with open arms, and for that we are very grateful.

I am your angel, and my name is Comforter. My essence is comfort, something that you give so very easily to others. You have such a beautiful way of offering comfort to those in need. You listen with an open heart. You look with eyes of love and understanding. You offer acceptance. You do not judge.

Comfort is so very badly needed in your world. There are so many who are struggling. Change is taking place at a head-spinning rate, and many are feeling the effects. This is why a gentle, comforting stance toward all those with whom one comes into contact is so necessary, especially at this time. Oh, to have a shoulder to cry on, a friend to talk to, or someone with whom to laugh over all the trials and tribulations of your busy and modern world.

The little comforts of life are so very important in your lives at this time also. A hot cup of tea, either enjoyed by yourself or with a companion. A soothing massage. A lavender bath. A foot rub. Touch, oh the importance of touch. This cannot be emphasized enough. A phone call to say, "I care." A welcoming "hello." A look that says, "I care about you." All these and more are the little comforts of life that make life worth living, that give it meaning.

Pam, you are such a talented woman. There is no doubt about that. Your law practice. Your dollhouse business. Your role as wife, mother, and friend. Your way of interacting with those on the council and in the community. In all these different roles, your ability to be the comforter has been manifested. I wish to tell you that I am proud of you, and I am proud to be your angel.

Perhaps you have not seen yourself in this light. That is not a bad thing. This has come to you quite naturally. And yet, it is I, your angel, who has been whispering in your ear and guiding you. And you have learned your lessons so very well. But then, learning comes so easily to one such as you, who is so very intelligent.

I wish to commend you. You have done a wonderful job of being the natural comforter that you are. You told Donna that you feel that you have lost the connection that you felt a number of years ago. Let me reassure you that the connection has not been lost at all. It has never left you. But it would behoove you to see this recent conversation and this letter as a little jump start, if you will. It is always beneficial to become more aware of one's connection to the spiritual realm. After all, you are Spirit.

So, my dear, please know this has been my true pleasure. I cannot tell you enough how very proud I am of you. Why, you would think I gave birth to you myself! Rest assured that I am always by your side, watching, guiding, and comforting, even as you comfort. Continue living your life with your current enthusiasm. Enjoy your puppy. What a joy! Please let me know if there is anything I can do. And ask!

With love and comfort,

Comforter

December 26, 2003

Dear Bob,

There are only a few more days left before a whole new year begins. I am so excited and happy that we are making this contact at this time. What a way for both of us to begin the year 2004! This is something that I have wanted to do for a long time, and now our time has come!

It is because of your openness to Donna that we are going to get to know one another. Actually, I know **you** very well. I am your angel, and my name is Paul. (Yes, you wanted a male angel, and **I am male**.) My maleness is very important to me. Why, I do not exactly know. We angels do not understand everything, just as you humans do not. Sometimes we just have to live with the questions and be okay with them.

My essence is dedication. I have been very dedicated to you, and as a result I have had to be very hardworking, as are you. You really have been quite hard to keep up with. You've had all these jobs, interests, hobbies, and travel experiences. Rest assured that whatever you have been involved in, so have I. By our very natures, we angels keep up with whatever it is that our humans get themselves involved in. And you have been quite a trip!

I am speaking somewhat tongue in cheek, but only to a point. You have been so very dedicated to your wife, to your family, and to being a very good provider. This has taken its toll on you, as you are aware. It is good that you are working only one job now. I would really like to see you take better care of yourself. You really need to put some of your own needs before the needs of others. Others, as you know, are relying upon you a great deal. You need to see to your own needs, as well as the needs of others.

This I cannot stress to you enough. Please apply your sense of dedication to yourself. Please think and pray on this. Ask yourself: How can I serve myself? What can I do to bring happiness and a sense of fulfillment into my life? You have thought so much of your family's needs for all these years that you have not asked yourself these oh, so important questions. Remember the Good Shepherd's admonishment to love others as you love yourself. I could go on and on about this point but hope that enough has been said.

Dedication. What an important word and concept. When one is dedicated to something, some person, or some cause, he devotes his thoughts, heart, and energy toward that end. Dedication is necessary. It is the force that drives one to right action. It often implies hard work. It implies selflessness and commitment. Please know that I commend you for your dedication and hard work. Your family has indeed been blessed with such a devoted husband and father.

What I ask of you, Bob, is simply this: Please be open to my help and guidance. You know my name, and you believe in my existence. Please remember to talk to me each day. I am very dedicated to you and will do all that I can (which is a great, great deal) to help you, to guide you and, yes, to make your life easier. I love you so very much. All you need do is say my name. That gesture on your part gives me permission to act, to intercede, to respond. You are so dear to me. Yes, you've been hard to keep up with. But I must say I've been very dedicated to my cause and have done a very good job. Perhaps if you slow down just a bit, we can both take a rest! Again, I tease you just a little and hope you don't mind. I love your laughter and sense of humor. We are going to become very good friends. I can just feel it! I take leave of this letter, but I will never take leave of you. I am always, and I do mean **always,** by your side. Call upon me. Please.

Love and more love,

With a heart of dedication,

Paul

December 28, 2003

Dear Cookie,

As Donna sits to type, she can sense my essence of peacefulness. She feels peaceful and at one with the goodness of this world that God the Creator has made. This is what God wants for all of his children, an abiding sense of peace and the knowing that All is Well, for indeed, All is Well.

My name is Abigail, and I am your angel. To be able to talk to you makes me so very happy that I want to cry. Oh, how my heart has ached to make this connection with you, one that you will not doubt or question. My heart has longed to reach out to you and to touch you, to ease your pain, and to lift your spirits. You are so very sweet and have strived all your life to be happy, to bring happiness to others (especially your husband and children), and to draw close to God. Let me reassure you that God is indeed very close to you and yours, and He also is happy that we are going to get to know one another.

There is an awful lot we could say about peace. Peace, it is well known, must begin in the heart of each individual. From there it must reach out to touch the hearts and lives of those with whom you live. Then, it must move out in an ever-expanding circle until it encompasses the whole world. So much can be accomplished through prayer to bring peace to one's own heart, to one's family or close circle that is considered family, to one's nation, and to the world. It is imperative at this time that all people everywhere see the world as family, the family of God. For indeed there is only one God, and all people on the face of the earth are one family.

My dear, dear Cookie, you have had more than your share of physical problems, more than your share of pain. And yet, your heart has remained very strong. You have not lost your sense of family, as evidenced by your willingness to gather family at Christmas in your home, even though this has been physically difficult for you. You never cease to extend love to your children, to experience joy in their successes, and to rejoice when they are able to be with you. Your love of family has brought you joy, a sense of fulfillment and, yes, peace.

I simply want to let you know that I have always been with you. I have seen your pain, but I have also seen your joy. Please know that I am only a word away and that word is my name. You obviously have seen that my name is closely related to your given name of Gail, which I think is very beautiful. I hope you like my name as well, as I love it. We get to choose our own names when we make this contact with our humans through Donna. I thought long and hard about my choice, and Abigail sounds so very right to me.

Your husband Bob, your sweet mother, your devoted children and I all love you so very much. Please ask me to help you with anything and everything. Your quilts are so very beautiful and are an extension of your heart of love. They will be treasured for many years to come. Continue to give your heart in this way. May peace continue to reign in your heart and in your family. I know you love God and have a huge heart of love for all humankind. Please pray for peace in your nation and the world. Please ask me to remind you to pray. Your prayers are needed and are very powerful.

I love you so. Know I am always close. Please call upon me.

With love and peace in my heart,

Abigail

Down-to-Earth Angels

Cookie's response:

Before Donna introduced me to my angel, Abigail, I knew very little about angels. I knew my daughter had a guardian angel. When she was very, very young, she fell down the uncarpeted basement steps. She was holding some glass bottles as she fell. My daughter did not get hurt in any way and the bottles were intact. She has since traveled the world, and without her guardian angel with her, I don't know how she could have survived some of the most difficult situations she found herself in.

What I knew about angels was quite basic. I knew angels were mentioned in the Bible. I knew people prayed to certain angels for certain situations.

On Christmas Day, I was discussing with Donna a saying I used when I was very sick. I have bi-polar disorder and suffer from severe depression. I had read in a book the saying: All is Well. I thought perhaps it was in the Bible. I repeated this saying over and over to myself and it helped me get through some rough times. Still, I did not know where I had read it. I eagerly accepted Donna's offer of a letter from my angel. I was amazed that in my letter Abigail said: All is Well.

I continued to doubt that Abigail was really my angel. One day I was feeling terrible, but I was determined to find out where I had originally read: All is Well. I asked Abigail to please help me find my saying in a quick fashion. I did not pick up the Bible first; instead, I chose another book I read a lot when I was sick. I started to page through this book. On the third page and again on the fifth page, I found "All is Well' a total of fifteen times. The book has 250 pages. I told Abigail, "Okay! Okay! Enough already. I believe! I believe!"

Oh, and one more thing. I found a great new quilt store. It's named Abigail.

December 29, 2003

Dear Steve,

Greetings! It is indeed my pleasure, sir, to make this contact with you. It is long overdue. You and I have had to be very patient with your sister-in-law, Donna. But the wait is now behind us...and away we go!

Wow! That tree was surely a big one! I had to get permission from the Man Upstairs to allow that to fall on your house. But you see, I was getting impatient and didn't know how to get through to you. We took so many things into consideration before we let that happen. For one thing, you and your beloved Ginny both know how to make lemonade from lemons; you can (for the most part) keep a cool head when faced with calamities; and you are very good at working with insurance companies and getting your due. So, considering all this, we decided that letting the tree fall on your house was in your best interest. Hey, you heard my name loud and clear. You were not afraid to tell Ginny, "Tony talked to me. He said, 'It's only wood.'"

So, the connection has been made. You know that I am your angel and that I am with you all the time. You also know that my essence is Unconditional Friendliness. Isn't that perfect? Unconditional Friendliness. You are one of the friendliest guys on the face of the planet and know how to make **everyone** feel right at home. Your heart goes out to others, as does your smile, your handshake or hug, and your friendly greeting. One is immediately comfortable in your presence. What the world needs now is—friendliness, friendliness, friendliness. More with your quality of friendliness would do a whole lot for the planet. Friendliness is quite contagious!

I cannot tell you how pleased I am that you quit smoking, Steve. This is something that you have wanted for a long time. And for you to publicly acknowledge that it was your angel who helped you quit is so powerful. I cannot tell you what it means to us angels when one of ours admits to others that we were of help. Why, it just opens the door for others to believe in our existence and to believe that we can help with so many things in your lives, even something as difficult as addictions. So, I applaud you and I thank you from the bottom of my heart.

Speaking of hearts, I want you to know that I recognize that you have a heart of gold. More gold than the gold chain you wear around your neck. A very pure and rich gold. A rare kind of gold. You have so much love inside of you—for your wife, daughters, son-in-law and beautiful granddaughters, Morgan and Mackenzie. The countless thoughtful things you do for your loved ones day in and day out are something to behold. Your family, you must be aware, would indeed be lost without you. Your friendly, jovial presentation of yourself is simply the outer expression of all the love that is inside you. You are a marvel to behold.

Please know that I see that this love reaches beyond your immediately family members. It reaches out to include extended family members. You open your heart and home and welcome family in without hesitation, not minding the extra work that these visits present. Know that your efforts are noticed and appreciated, on this side as well as that. Friends at the bar are always glad when you are around. Why wouldn't they be? You lift their spirits, make their hearts glad, and they know they have a friend to talk to.

I could go on and on. You make my heart glad. Just to think of you and to be with you brings me great joy! Know that I am **always** with you. Always. As you care for your wife, children, and grandchildren. As you go about your shopping and household work. As you visit in the bar. Always!

I really don't want to close, but don't have a whole lot more to say at this time. I'm glad the wait is over and that I've had a chance to talk to you. Please keep conversing with me day in and day out. Nothing would please me more. I am here to serve you and long to do so.

With a heart of love,

With a love for friendliness,

Tony

Donna Allen

January 2, 2003

Dear Lois*,

You are brave to let Donna write this letter to you, even though you doubt that you have any angel at all. Let me reassure you, my darling, that I am alive and well and have your best interest at heart. That is the way I have been communicating with you all these years—through your heart.

Let me introduce myself to you. My name is Suzanna, and my essence is freedom. As Donna explained to you, an angel's essence is very closely correlated to a person's highest potential. You are a very free-spirited person. You laugh readily, are accepting of great differences among people, and always give others the benefit of the doubt. In other words, you allow people to be who they are without passing judgment on them. This is something that you take for granted. Yet, it truly is a gift.

You have lived many different places around the world. France. Italy. Hong Kong. The United States has not really felt like home to you. In some ways, you have felt like you haven't had a home. And yet I tell you that you do indeed have a home and that your heart is your home. Your heart is something you take with you wherever you go. So in a sense, you take your home with you wherever you go. This might sound a little farfetched to you. Yet I reassure you that this is true. The person without a connection to his or her heart center is the person without a home.

Let us make the connection between a person's heart and freedom. When one lives from his or her heart center, he or she has clear guidance available all the time. The heart was designed to act as a compass, leading one to happiness and fulfillment. This does not leave the head, or reason, out of the picture. The mind and logic certainly have their place in all of this. But it is the heart that is the "heart of the matter." The heart is like a guiding light. It leads one to the truth of one's being. It leads one to Love, which is of God. And when one lives a life of love, one is free.

Many do not realize that God is nothing but Love. God does not judge. God does not punish. And God certainly does not condemn. One is allowed to choose and to learn from his or her mistakes. Yes, "sin" is but a spiritual error. And doesn't one often learn best that which is learned from making mistakes? Each human on the face of planet Earth is created as a completely free being. Free to make choices and decisions. Free to fall down and get back up again, and again, and again, if necessary. If God did not give to all the freedom of choice, then all of you would be as puppets on strings. This is not what God desired for His masterpiece creation, Humankind.

More could be said about God's all-important decision to create all people as free beings. But what I wish to tell you, Lois, is that **you** are free. You are free to live your life completely as you choose. You are free to invite me into your life, which I hope so very much you will do. You must ask for me to be in your life for me to be active. You are free to tell me that you would much rather I stay in the background as I have, and there I must stay. Please know that I am with you each and every day and night. I see all that you do. I see and feel the laughter in your voice, which lifts the spirits of others. I watch as you practice your cello, as your get your massages, as you prepare your meals. Yes, I see **everything,** and **I love you so!**

I beseech you not to doubt my existence, my love for you, or my ability to be active in your life. Live your life! You are free! You are my delight! May your friendship with

Donna Allen

Donna continue for another seventeen years and seventeen after that. You have been good for each other, and she has learned a great deal from you about freedom. You are blessed to have known each other for such a long time, since your children were babes and together you pushed them in strollers down your street.

I don't want to close. I want to go on talking forever. Hopefully we will! Know I am **always** here for you.

So much love to you and your family,

With an appreciation for your free-spirited nature,

Suzanna

January 4, 2004

My dear, dear Susan,

Please know there is never **anything** to fear when you open yourself to receive my messages. I would never say anything that would cause your heart to hurt more than it already does. It has hurt so much of the time since Leah was taken from your arms of love. I want only to comfort you and your dear family, to give you counsel when needed, and to express this deep love that I hold for you.

For the sake of others, I will share that my essence is Motherliness. You came to know my name through spirit communication. Although no confirmation was necessary, it came nonetheless. Our relationship has been growing with each passing day, as has your relationship with your beloved daughter, Leah, who is now with the angels in heaven. She is indeed a blessing to all of us on this side of the veil, Susan. I cannot stress that enough to you.

We are all so thrilled that you were open to the healing session with your dear mother yesterday. The healings took place on so many levels, some of which you and your mother have not yet recognized. Your mother, Donna, was open to my promptings to offer the session and you were open to healing, even though it was at first a little scary for you. I was present throughout, as Donna explained to you. It was the Father Himself who did the healing. The forgiveness work you have done in your mother-daughter relationship was acknowledged and commended by your mother. I commend you, too, my dear. Forgiveness is not always easy, but it is necessary. Your mother was so young when she had you and your twin sister. She has learned so much and is still learning to get her head out of the clouds and to stay grounded. She has more work to do in this area.

Leah is thrilled that the two of you communicated so much during your session. She did indeed choose to come to you and your beloved husband as she did. She did want to advance, as she said. Many, many angels do come to her for advice all the time. She has felt human pain. She understands as others who have not been in human form cannot. She still misses you, her father, and her brother. But she really is fine. She loves to fly to visit Michael, and he is very good to her. Mary cares for her constantly. She is our delight on this side of the veil. As she said, she has many gifts to give to **all** of you, and they will continue throughout your lifetimes. She was so blessed to be born into your whole family. She gave all of you so much love, but she received so much love as well. This love will never be forgotten or die. It will be a part of all of you forever.

You have such a sweet and loving way about you. You are sensitive to the needs and feelings of others. You offer comfort and support and kind words. You listen with your heart. Your highest potential is indeed motherliness, and the way you care for all children who are left to your care is something to behold. Wasn't it marvelous the way Leah made her presence known to you with the music and flying snow of the Precious Moments ball? She does not want you to doubt for one minute that **she is with you.** Why, she has so many on this side pulling for you that you'd think you were the only person there who needed support! I tease a bit. She is only being the loving being that she is. She is kind of like the little princess here. Everyone loves her, admires her, comes to her, and dotes on her. Talk about precious!

Susan, please know that you are a **wonderful** mother to Tyler. He is indeed very smart, intuitive, and sensitive. To say that he is active would be an understatement. He will excel in sports and you and Jim will be **running** to keep up with him. But neither of you will mind, certainly not Jim. You will share much joy as a family. And we on this side rejoice in family harmony and joy.

Leah loves when you talk to her, just as she loves when Grandma Bratton talks to her. She loves your mom, and you know the feeling is mutual. She will always remember how her grandfathers held her and loved her. Beth, too. As you know, all who held her felt her essence of love radiating from her tiny body. As Mary Lou Beers said, "Oh my, you can feel the love coming from this child!" All who were within her radius of love, which extended far beyond that of a normal child, felt her love and were affected by it. Love is so powerful. Leah, as sweet and innocent as she is, is powerful in her own right. The power of love will become known on the face of the earth, and it **will** be changed forever.

Thank you for being so open. You have many gifts which wish to express themselves. May our love for one another continue to grow, and grow, and grow. I am always close. We are all always close. I take leave of you knowing full well that we will continue to be in touch. Leah's angel, Christine, would like to be included in this letter. As you know, she is always near you, and you may talk to her as well. She is a very sweet angel.

With a heart full of love and tenderness,

With the heart of a mother,

Josephine

Susan's response:

Donna Allen

I experienced so much from my letter that it is difficult to put it into words. If I had to sum it up...I felt an overwhelming, powerful, joyous, unconditional love full of unlimited hope.

January 24, 2004

Dear Libby*,

Let me tell you first off that Donna has sensed my excitement about writing to you. My heart is doing pitter-patters at the thought of us becoming good friends and communicating with each other. We are all so happy that you were open to Donna at school. Since you two first met, you have felt that the two of you were kindred spirits. That link is real and meaningful and is the reason I am talking with you through this means at this time. Again I applaud you for being open to something about which you were unsure. You asked for a sign that you might know whether or not Donna's gift is indeed of God. You hung in there, hoping against hope, until the end of the service when the words about us angels came to you and touched your heart. You knew that you were not deviating from God's plan for you in this matter. Caution is always a good thing in matters of the spirit. One must trust in his or her own guidance. What is right for one is not necessarily right for another, and each must proceed at his or her own pace.

I am thrilled to introduce myself to you. My name is Francine. I hope you like my name. You see, we angels get to choose our own names. We want our humans to be able to call out to us, so that we can come running when we hear it. Actually, we don't need to come running, because we are **always** close by. I have long awaited this moment. This I cannot stress enough. One thing we angels **must** have when it comes to relating to our humans is a great, great deal of patience. You see, I cannot act without your permission. You have a free will, as you know. God created you as such. You are free to choose your own thoughts, words, and actions. You are free to accept God into your life or to reject Him. You know that you strive to be in

God's will all the time. Sometimes you question whether or not what you are doing is what God wants you to do. Let me reassure you of God's great love for you, and how very pleased He is that it is your desire to do His will. Your very desire to do the will of God is such a sweet fragrance to us angels. We desire to do God's will as well.

My essence is patience. In other letters, Donna has written about the connection between a person's highest potential and the essence of that person's angel, who was so very carefully chosen for him or her. Yes, I was carefully chosen for you with the idea in mind that I could help you grow into a very patient and loving individual. Libby, you have done exactly this, but I would like you to see yourself in this light. Your sweet, cheerful greetings to others. Your kind and encouraging words. The warm touch you offer. Your ready smile. All of this and more are expressions of your patience.

Patience, more than any other virtue, is one that must be cultivated. It is to be highly prized. Some might see patience as weakness or as the inability to act. Yet, oftentimes patience is required for God's plan to manifest. Often it is necessary to "wait upon the Lord." Waiting can be very difficult in a culture such as yours where "Just Do It" has become the motto. But when one decides to "Let Go and Let God," there is often a period of time before the good which one seeks is made manifest. It would be easy during this time of waiting for one to doubt, to think that God has not answered the prayer, to take matters into one's own hands. God understands all of this as any loving father would. But God does indeed bless the one who stands firm in faith and with **patience** awaits the perfect outcome for all concerned. May all humans grow in patience. May they grow in patience with themselves and their own shortcomings and weaknesses. May they grow in patience with each other, even as they grow in love for one another. And may they grow in patience as God's perfect plan for their lives is made manifest.

My dear Libby, I cannot tell you enough how much I love you. I truly do know everything about you and have been with you since your took your first breath. I will be with you until you are no longer on the physical plane. Please, oh please, let me be your friend. You can talk to me about anything. Just as a loving mother cares deeply about all that concerns her child, so do I care deeply about all that concerns you. I am very, very powerful. There is so much I can do to bring about good in your life. Please give me the power to act in your life by asking me for whatever it is you desire. I am always here to help, protect and guide you. I want to be your **very** best friend.

My love to you and your dear family,

Francine

February 1, 2004

Dear Libby*,

In your note to Donna you said: Tell me how I can talk to Francine directly. We on this side of the veil have been laughing with joy over your request. Donna has typed almost forty letters for others, but you are the first one who has asked this of her. Good for you! We angels love to communicate with our humans. It gives us such joy.

If you don't mind, we are going to be talking in general about communicating with us angels. Talking to us is very much like talking to God, or to your higher self, or to anyone out there whom you think might be listening. And rest assured that each thought, each sigh, each prayer, each desire that you send our way is heard. **Nothing** that is sent our way passes without catching our attention. Indeed, we sit and wait for a word. We wait for the music, the sweet music, which is the voice of our beloved.

So, you can talk to Francine all the time and trust that you are being heard and loved. Perhaps what you would like to know is how you can hear back, how you can feel and know her presence in your life. This is something that often takes a little bit more practice, as do all things of the spirit. Just as God is always close and hears each prayer and word, it takes an attentive stance and growth in faith to hear His sweet voice, to discern His guidance, to feel His presence.

At this time, Donna does not know how to act as a mediator between others and their angels. There are indeed some who have this gift. What she does have to offer you, though, is her own experience with her dear angel, Marc. Most people, I might add, have many angels who are working on their behalf. However, it is advised to get to know and communicate with one's primary angel before being concerned about the others. A primary angel has the ability to consult with other angels to the benefit of the beloved. This is done often on this side. We all work together and have much to offer each other.

It was very exciting to Donna when she realized that Marc was communicating with her through "automatic writing." We on this side sometimes refer to this as "writing with your own hand." This type of communication is available to all. You simply sit with paper and pencil or pen in hand, take a deep breath, ask your angel to communicate to you through this means, and let the words flow onto the paper. It might help if you visualize your angel actually doing the writing, as if your angel is the one who is holding the writing utensil. It is important for you to feel comfortable with whatever visualization you choose, if indeed you choose one at all. One can also write automatically onto a keyboard.

I, Francine, can make my presence known to you by your making requests of me. For example, you might ask me to "smooth out your day." At the end of the day, you might sit back and observe just how smoothly things have gone. You might ask me to guide you to the next book you might read about angels, and lo and behold, the answer will become very obvious. Words like "please show me," "please guide me," and "please help me" will bring a quick response. Know that I will rush to make my presence known to you, dear, sweet Libby. Our communication might not be as direct as you would like at first, but it will be real and meaningful, just as your communications with your beloved Jesus are so very real.

Let all of us angels mention one more means of communication at this time. There is what is called "inner listening." Oftentimes when we speak to our humans, they think that what they hear is perhaps just their imagination. This is because often what they hear sounds like their own voice to them. They mistakenly think that the voice they hear should be distinct from their own. This is not true. One must carefully listen to the message. Very often it will sound like you are just talking to yourself. We are so closely linked to our humans that often what they are thinking and what we are advising are one and the same. But let it be known that we are **separate beings** from you. We each have our own personalities, likes and dislikes. Some of us take our jobs more seriously than others. We fret over those who "slack off," believe you me, and we take steps to correct them. Rest assured, most of us are very highly qualified!

Just as any relationship takes time to grow and develop, so it is with one's angel. At first one might question, even doubt. This is normal. But be persistent. The veil is indeed becoming thinner and thinner with each passing day. More and more people believe in our existence, our power, and our love. There is so much power in love, and that is what this relationship between us angels and our humans is all about—love.

So, our dear Libby, we hope this communication has helped. It is the best that Donna has to offer at this time, and she is hoping that it will suffice. She has spent time developing her relationship with Marc these past two years, and it has become a very important part of her life. We might add that this relationship is very, very special to

Marc as well. We all love you so much. We appreciate your request beyond measure.

With love and gratitude,

Francine, your beloved angel

The Angelic Realm

February 15, 2004

Dear Jennifer,

Hi there! It is so nice to make your acquaintance. This is long overdue, but I can live with that fact now that we are having this contact. Your chat with Donna in the teachers' lounge was timely and planned. We think both of you know this.

Yes, my name is Charles and my essence is persistence. Donna keeps sensing that I am a very large angel, and that is correct. Some on this side tease me and say that I am a "giant." But I don't mind. I am very, very large and my size, if some of you saw me, might frighten you. But let me reassure you that I am as soft on the inside as a pussycat. Some on this side call me "Pussycat" because of my gentle nature. You may call me what you like. It really doesn't matter to me at all.

Donna really already told you all that you need to know about us angels. We see what is the highest and best in you and focus on that. We are not about to point out your faults or weaknesses. Why, you humans know those all too well and actually tend to focus your attention on them instead of on your goodness and strengths. And, as the saying goes, "what you focus your attention on increases." So, it our privilege and "job," you might say, to focus on all that is good, all that is positive. So, we really have a very nice "job."

Some think that we angels do not and cannot know what it is like to live in your world, and to some extent this is true. We do not have to live in the trenches as you do, and tend to see things from our lofty position. Yet, let us reassure you that we care deeply about you, all of you, and are constantly on the lookout to find ways to help, to understand,

and to manifest our powers in your lives. Do not underestimate us and what we can do in your lives. We **persist** in our work of helping you to make your lives all that they can be.

Yes, **persistence** is a quality that we angels possess. We must persist in our work because there are forces at work in your culture that run counter to what God wants for all of you. We won't go into the details of all that. It is just so obvious; I don't want to waste my time talking about it. You, Jennifer, get upset about all the things you see in your country that are going wrong. You have a right to be upset. So, **persist** in doing what you believe is necessary to right the wrongs. **Persist** in expressing your opinions and "carrying your signs."

Do you know how proud I am of you? You have the warmest heart. Yes, you yell a lot, make a lot of noise and sometimes frighten others. But underneath that gruffness is a big, soft, gentle heart and a lot of goodness. So, you see, we have a lot in common, don't we? See what a great team we are? What do you say that we go forward that way—as a united front, as a team, as friends?

We are all so happy that you thought that what Donna had to say was "so cool"! We think that we are pretty cool, too, and we are happy that we are finally able to make our presence and power known in a way that is bigger and better than ever before. These are exciting times in which to be living. Yes, these are challenging times, but we would rather focus on the fact that these are exciting times as well.

Please, oh please, remember what Donna said: You must **ask** for my help, my guidance, my assistance, my protection, etc. You have a free will. I cannot and will not interfere with that great gift of God. So, please, remember to ask. **Persist** in your asking, and I promise you, I will deliver.

That's about all for now. When I have no more to say, I just quit talking. I love you. I love you. I love you. (Pass it on!)

Love, Love, Love,

Charles (Pussycat)

The Angelic Realm

April 21, 2004

Dear Beth,

How appropriate that I should be writing to you on this, your 18th birthday! Happy birthday, my dear.

Your sweet mother has already told you that my name is Christopher, and my essence is strength and courage. I am your newly born son's angel, and he and I will be having quite a journey together.

I will not be telling you anything about Aiden's future. That is not the purpose of us angels. My purpose is to guide Aiden along his life's path, to be at his side at all times, protecting, loving, and offering reassurance and encouragement at every turn.

I cannot tell you how excited I am about this "assignment." Yes, I volunteered and accepted with enthusiasm to be with Aiden on his life's journey. He is a wonder to behold. He is strong in character. Honor, integrity and freedom are very important to him, and I will be nurturing these qualities in him. Of course, strength and courage go hand in hand with these other qualities. They all go together; they intermingle, if you will. As his mother, it is important that you notice these characteristics developing and nurture their blossoming in him. Opportunities will present themselves whereby he will be able to express these qualities and, thus, his highest self.

I tell you this only to give you a little "heads up." All the love this little guy exudes is something to behold, isn't it? Those who hold him cannot help but feel joyful and in touch with all that is good in the Universe. The love you and Ben share with each other and for Aiden brings joy to all of us on this side of the veil.

Please know that you can talk to me on Aiden's behalf at any time. We angels have such a special place in our hearts for those in our care. I can call upon all the angels anytime I feel the need for extra support. So can you, my dear. **Do not hesitate** to call...Christopher! **Do not hesitate** to call...Angels! We will come running to your side to be with you, with Ben, with Aiden, and with all those whom you hold dear. We love you so very much. Know that Annabelle, Hamilton, and I are all friends. We communicate with one another and are here for all of you and working on your behalf night and day.

So much joy lies ahead for all of you. We share in your concerns, yes. We share in your joy, laughter, and happiness. Soon you will be able to communicate with us through your mother. In the meantime, know that you are heard. Know that you are loved. Know that you are one with God and the universe. Know that you are love.

With love beyond measure,

Christopher

May 22, 2004

Dear Katie,

I, my dear, am your very special angel, and I am **so** happy and excited to be writing to you. My name is Jezzebelle. That might seem like an unusual name for an angel, and perhaps it is an unusual spelling; but I quite like it and I hope it makes you laugh. You see, I just love your laughter. It is such good medicine for you and others. For me too!

My essence is gaiety. My essence is closely related to your highest potential. There isn't really a whole lot I need to say to you. Perhaps this is because I feel that we communicate at the heart level all the time. I just want you to know that I am very close to you and to Joey all the time. He is such a sweetheart, and I see how much you love him. He delights in your love for him and your dear husband, and I delight in your love as well.

Joey's angel's name is Gertrude. Yes, he has a female angel. She is the sweetest thing and just loves Joey to pieces. Please be sure to call upon her on Joey's behalf. She would do anything for him, as I would do for you.

I also want you to know that you are living your life in a very balanced fashion. You have a wonderful career and are giving of yourself to your students. Your marriage is happy. You take time for family and friends. You also take some time for yourself, which is so very important. Try to remember in your busy life that it is very important that you consider your needs first of all. You deserve to give yourself all of the love that you need. As your cup overflows, you will give of your excess and will not deplete yourself of that which you need to keep healthy, strong, and active.

We in the angelic realm delight in serving our humans. I am so thrilled that you are my charge. I have **always** delighted in your being, in your sweet, happy, and generous nature. We have a long and happy future together. Know that I am with you always. Know that I can and do communicate with Gertrude and that our relationship is a happy and loving one. God is good. God is good. Rest in the knowledge that all is well.

Love, peace, and blessings,

Jezzebelle

Katie's response:

Donna,

Thank you so much for my angel letter. Being a new, "first-time" mom, it is so comforting to hear these words! At the time I received the letter, I was actually trying to teach Joey to sleep through the night. At my pediatrician's suggestion, I was trying "tough love" (as I call it)—letting him cry for five, ten or fifteen minutes at a time after putting him to bed, hoping that he'd learn to comfort himself and fall asleep. This was *grueling* for me.

I would sit and cry outside his door as he lay crying, sometimes screaming. Well, after only three days, the doctor's advice paid off. Joey was sleeping pretty well through the night. But your words from Jezzebelle were very comforting. It was wonderful to know about Joey's guardian angel. If I couldn't be there physically comforting him, it was great to know that Gertrude could. Thanks again, Katie

May 24, 2004

My dear, sweet Margaret*,

I am your guardian angel, and my name is J. J. Please call me that, although my "given" name is Jonathan James. My essence is calmness and openness. These two qualities are related, as we shall see. There is so much that I want to say to you, so much that I would like to talk to you about. I have truly been excited about writing to you since that conversation between you and Donna in the teachers' lounge.

Let me tell you first off that I chose to be with you and have been with you since your birth. I will be with you until you make your transition, in other words, for the rest of your earthly life. You are such a sweet person, and that sweetness is what people observe about you at first meeting. Others, like Donna, observe your openness to that which might seem "different" to others. It is your openness that led to the conversation about us angels and Doreen Virtue's book *Healing with the Angels.*

Doreen has done us a **huge** favor and has connected many people with the angelic realm. There are so many people who are now **open** to the idea of our existence, and the bridge between your world and ours in now in its final stages of construction. It takes a genuine **openness** on the part of an individual to let go of past resistance to the unseen world and to believe in what cannot at this time be perceived with the human eye. Of course, some humans can see us. But in the near future more and more humans will be seeing us and delighting in our newfound relationships. So, I wish to commend you, my dear, for being **open** to that which you cannot see. Your simple interest in these matters has led you to this point and to **me!**

Calmness is a quality that is not to be taken lightly, **especially** in a society such as yours where so many seem to be running helter skelter. Yet, you, my sweetheart, have a lightness, a sweetness about you that helps others who are in your presence feel a sense of calm, of stillness. This is such a wonderful trait. I, too, am very calm, very serene. This peace, this calm, is born of a trust in the Divine, in the goodness of creation, a knowing that All is Well in the World. Oh sure, you've got lots of problems on planet Earth. Yet, it **is** possible for one to experience peace on earth, even if there is chaos all around, which there is. The peace, the calm, the stillness is within and is something that cannot be taken away from you without your permission. Your openness to that which is unseen gives you access to this peace that is beyond all understanding.

So, my dear, we have made this connection. I love you so very much. Please do talk to me all the time. I can hear everything you say and think. I watch your every move and am always standing nearby ready to answer your call. You are like a special poem to me. (I happen to love poetry.) You and I are one, just as you are one with all that is in the beautiful universe. We are ever so close.

All my love and admiration,

J.J.

May 28, 2004

Dear Paula*,

Aha! So glad we have the chance to meet! You have an open heart to things of the spirit, which is why I am speaking to you at this time. It is going to be so much fun, my dear, so much fun!

My name is Glenda, and I am your "primary" angel. Now, please know that you have lots of angels. But I am "top dog" you might say. I can enlist the help of other angels if I need to, and rest assured that I will not hesitate to call upon others as needed.

Some might think that I have a strong personality or that perhaps I am a little outspoken. So be it. The angelic world needs all kinds of angels, just as your world needs all kinds of people. There are different jobs for different people, or in our case, different jobs for different angels. My essence, one might say, is the ability to be emphatic. I like to give great emphasis to that which I think is important. I'm not wishy-washy and haven't a whole lot of tolerance for those who are. It's important, I believe, to know where one stands on issues and to make one's opinions known. Others are free to express their opposing opinions to me, and I delight in that. But please, oh please, just don't have no opinion at all. There are so many pressing issues, and it is important that people think about them and then act on their convictions.

Okay. So I've had my say. You, my dear, truly have your head on straight. You know what is important to you and you let your opinions be known. Let's take your work, for example. You know that living skills are very important. How many students have you taught to cook, to sew, to balance a checkbook? How many young people have cared for a "pretend" crying baby in order that they might begin to understand the pressures of a new little one? **These are important skills!** Why is the importance of these skills minimized in your schools when they are so applicable to daily living? Believe you me, your schools had better make a direct link between what is being taught and what needs to be learned and what is relevant, or the young will become even more unhappy and disruptive.

Paula, I want you to know that I am very proud of you. You are an outstanding mother and teacher. You truly care. You take the time to accomplish what is important to you. You have set a very good example for your children and for those in your care in your classrooms.

Perhaps I seem a little harsh or abrasive. Know that I am Love, as are you. Know that I care deeply about you, those whom you love, and the career to which you have dedicated yourself. I am at your service. Please ask to for guidance, for help in any and all areas of your life. I will rush to your side. The truth of the matter is, I am **always** by your side, longing to be of service to you.

With a heart full of love for you and yours,

Glenda

Paula's response:

Donna,

I want to thank you for your gift to me! I have always been taught and believed there was an angel there for me, but it was so great to get some affirmation! Ever since I read her letter, I have felt much calmer about everything going on around me and much more appreciative of everyone in my life.

Glenda has been a *conscious* part of my life since I received her letter. I found a little angel figurine recently that has become part of my "kitchen décor." I call it Glenda and it helps remind me of my Glenda! So, thank you! Paula

June 10, 2004

My dear Noel,

This is such a very special moment for me. I get to talk with you! My energy is boundless. So is yours. We are going to talk about that for just a moment, in just a moment.

My name is Henrietta and my essence is love and sweetness, something you are very familiar with, at home with. You are very loving and very sweet, also. This is an indication that we have been working together for a very long time, even if you were not consciously aware of it. The more a person resembles his or her angel, the greater the indication that s/he has been open to the guidance, the whisperings, the nudges and promptings of his or her angel. You have been very open all these years and have, thus, brought me great joy.

Energy is something that humans feel is in short supply these days. So many are saying, "I just don't have the energy I used to." "I don't have enough energy." "If only I felt more energetic…" But, you see, energy is not in short supply. It is just that humans, too many of them, are using their energy, their precious energy, for the wrong things. Too many are doing things they don't really want to be doing and for the wrong reasons. It is so important that each person follows the promptings of his or her heart, listens to inner guidance and acts upon what s/he is guided to do. So many are following the ways of your society, which promotes constant motion, constant doing, and constant interaction.

What is so desperately needed is for humans to take quiet time, to contemplate, to meditate, if you will. It is through the heart that one connects with the Divine, with his or her inner wisdom and highest self. Yet, this is not something that is taught in your culture. Oh, some are getting the message, but not enough. Don't be one of those who do not take time to get to know their truest longings and truest desires. Take time to live in the silence, to appreciate nature, and to connect with all that is true and good and sweet within yourself and in your world.

When Donna told you that my essence is love and sweetness, your heart melted. You felt a connection with those words because that is **Who You Are**. You were making a connection with your highest self. You've had a feeling glimpse of me. You know that I exist and am close. Let me reassure you that I am as real as the next tree you look at, or the next flower, or the next blade of grass. **I am real.** Please know this beyond a shadow of a doubt.

I am **always** close to you. I know the longings of your heart, your concerns, and your worries. Try not to worry. Bring your worries to me, and let me transform them into concerns upon which you can act and bring resolution. I can and desire to bring a light touch to your life. You are my sweetheart. You are my love.

Oh, your beautiful children, your beautiful children. May the Most High bless those already with you and the one in your womb. You are a most beautiful mother. Do take time to nurture yourself. A mother these days has so little time for herself. Yet, if you do not take care of yourself, who will? This is your most important task, to take care of yourself. Remember this. It is important.

I was most anxious to talk with you. Donna sensed this. Yet, I did not want her to feel any pressure to accomplish this task. She, too, is a mother as well as a grandmother, wife, friend, healer, writer, teacher, pet owner and so on.

She has learned (with a great deal of help from the spirit world) to put herself first. I know. I know. This sounds selfish to you, to so many of you. But I reassure you that this is the order of things. You must place yourself first. This is self-love. This is vital information. Please do not disregard it. Please take it to heart. Ask me to guide you in this area.

Phew! I feel better now. I've had this chance to talk with you, and, yes, I feel better. Take care, my love, take care. We'll be in touch. You can count on that.

I love you. I love you. I love you.

Henrietta

June 14, 2004

My dear Clar,

Here is the long-awaited letter. Donna has been bugging me about writing and did not want to wait any longer. She wanted you to receive this letter **before** your son's birthday, and I did not want to disappoint her.

My name is Timothy, and I want you to know that I've heard all of your prayers to me. Yes, my essence is assertiveness. Assertiveness is a very positive trait. Sometimes people confuse assertiveness with aggressiveness. There is a **huge** difference between these two qualities; they are not to be confused. Assertive is a positive, moving-forward force. It says: "I have something to say. I have something to do. This is important and I want to be listened to. I **will** be listened to. I **will** act in a manner that is right for me." It is respectful of the rights of others. It is also very, very respectful of the self.

One who is assertive automatically lets others know of his or her own confidence. This display of confidence begets confidence in all parties involved. From the spiritual perspective, it might be said that confidence in one's self, expressed as assertion, is a statement that one is one with the Divine, the Creator of All that Is.

You might be asking yourself how all of this relates to your beloved son, Eric, for whom you have so many concerns. Let me reassure you that there is an important connection. Eric is not an assertive person in most situations. He has the sweetest heart and the gentlest nature. He is such a gift to those who know him well, to those who can feel his softness and goodness. Let me reassure you that you have nothing to worry about for Eric. He is fine and will continue to be fine.

However, any little thing that you can do to encourage Eric to be a little more assertive would be helpful. Perhaps I should use the word "allow" instead of "encourage." We do not want Eric to believe that we think he should be any way other than the way he is now. His spirit would possibly interpret this as a criticism, which is the last thing that would be nurturing for him. There are, nonetheless, little signs of approval you can send his way to let him realize that he **can** assert himself, think for himself and do for himself. Let this approval be felt first of all in your heart. Your approving stance will then automatically express itself at various levels in the way that is most beneficial to Eric. In this situation, as in all situations, it is the heart attitude that is of primary importance. All else will flow from that. Your wholehearted approval of your beloved son will send the loving energy that is necessary for him to move into his highest potential his way.

All of you humans live in such a fast-paced, often competitive world. Often, those who cannot or choose not to keep up seem to be getting lost in the race. Eric is not lost in the race. This is because he is not competing. Good for him! He is being who he is, and God loves him for that. And God loves you, Clar, for being such a wonderful and loving mother. We all love you and your son (and your other children too, of course) so very much. We all feel your heart of love.

Stay on your spiritual path. Your energy is doing much to alleviate some of the negative, low-frequency energy on planet Earth. We love your world and take great joy in serving those who are dedicated to making it a better place for all, a heaven on Earth. This is possible! Heaven on Earth. Isn't that a happy thought? Cling to that thought as you love yourself, your Eric, your spiritual path and your God.

Please keep talking to all of us. We need you to help make your world all that God intended it to be.

With great love and undying appreciation,

Timothy and the Angelic Realm

Donna Allen

The following sweetheart of an angel, Gregory, came as quite a surprise. There's more on Neal in the third chapter.

June 23, 2004

Hey, Neal,

What d'ya say, ole pal? This letter ain't goin' be the easiest for Donna to type. Ya see, I speak a lit' bit different than all the other angels. Yup, it's true. But that's jist the way things are. My name, as Miss Donna already told ya, is Gregory. I do tend to be ver,' ver' independent. I just don't like it when nobody tells me what to do. Some folks up here think I'm a bit weird; but then, ya know, that's their problem. At least, that's the way I figger it.

But deep inside, I'm the most peace-lovin', love-lovin', and fun-lovin' guy around. Ain't nothin' wrong with that or with me, the way I see it. Gosh, yerself, Donna. Jist keep typin'.

See, Neal, I've been with ya all yer life. Ya haven't paid much mind to me, and that's okay. I don't really mind if someone ignores me. I figger that's just the way things need to be at the moment. But, now's the time, at least accordin' to my way of lookin' at things, for you and me to git to know one another a bit. That's if it's okay with you.

In my book, yer jist one helluva guy. Why, ya go around with that drum, makin' all kinda people happy and sad and growin' and some such things. I can't say that I understand all o' it myself. But I do see the end results. People are connectin' with their spirit guides and learnin' to love 'emselves and each other. Why, it's jist so beautiful, it makes my eyes water. Yup, tears jist well up in my eyes and run down my cheeks.

One thing we do have in common, ole pal, besides the independence, the love, the peace and the fun, is a greeeeaaat sense o' humor. There ain't nothin' better than a good chuckle or a good belly laugh. When people laugh, that tickle feelin' just goes all through their bodies. Their hearts sing; and well, the laughter jist plain does them a whole lot o' good. What yer world needs now is a whole lot of laughter; at least that's the way I see things.

Y'have a whole lot o' help from the spirit realm. Why, we're always vyin' for yer attention. Ya listen and respond and speak yer mind, and we all appreciate that, mind ya. But, if I could ask one favor of ya, it would be to turn yer thoughts to me, yer angel Gregory, jist a tad bit more often. I really do like attention, though I hate to admit it. Jist a little ole….Gregory, what do you think about this? Or, Hey, Gregory, would ya kindly show me what to do here?

I'll come arunnin', buddy. I'll come arunnin'. I'm like all the angels in that I want so much to be o' service. Service is the name of the game. I love to serve. I love to serve. See, we have a whole lot in common.

I'm signin' off for now. But please be in touch. Take one of yer journeys to visit with me, would ya please? I love ya, buddy. I love ya.

Gregory

June 28, 2004

My dear Shar,

Ever since Donna prayed for you at the prayer meeting, I've been hoping that you two would meet and have a chance to talk. What a perfect setting: a campfire, the company of your beautiful dogs, and sweet Aiden. Indeed, last night's meeting was planned.

My name is Marianna. I love my name. I was told to choose a name when I learned that I would be making this contact with you. I hope you love it, too. Please call my name often. Oh, please do that for me, would you? My essence is cheerfulness. The type of cheerfulness of which I am made is one that is born of a deep and abiding trust in the goodness of God, the universe, and your world. My face is not a phony, cheery one—one that smiles all the time even if there is sorrow or hurt inside. No, my face is cheery because I know there is reason to be of good cheer: There is a God of love who cares for all of His creation and who communicates that love in so many, many ways.

You have experienced this love of God so much recently—since your diagnosis of cancer. The little and big signs you've had—that God is good, that God is close, and that God cares for so very much for you—are very real. These signs are not your active imagination or simply your longings being given expression. No, they are, all of them, God's way of saying, "You are my beloved, Shar. I am taking good care of you and your loved ones. You are mine and I am yours. Rest in my loving arms. Bring all your concerns to me. Share your tears with me. And please share your joys with me as well."

Your heart is so open, Shar. You are growing; this is true. But what you cannot fully see is how much you are touching the lives of all those around you. Your faith, your cheerfulness, your courage, your light, your smiles and your laughter are such good medicine for all those in your circle of influence. You are helping others to grow, to reach deep within for all that is truest and wisest within themselves.

The love you and your daughter share is so very beautiful, so very special. We are all happy that the two of you have this very special bond that will last for all eternity. I've asked the Most High to bless the little child within her womb. Blessed be. And so it is. You've sensed a growing closeness with all your loved ones. May this increasing closeness continue to bring you comfort and joy. I cannot tell you enough how very special you are—to me and to all those who know and love you.

One thing Donna failed to mention to you in your conversation last evening is the importance of asking me for whatever it is you want or need. God created you with a free will, and I can act only with your permission, at your request. So, my sweetheart, I will be waiting and hoping. Please ask me to help you or serve you as often as you would like. That truly is my role in your life—to be of service to you. Should you desire to know more fully the depth of my love and commitment to you, just ask. Should you need comfort or guidance, just ask. Should you desire help for a loved one, just ask. The signs that I am present and able to assist you will be unmistakable to you, as you have your heart and ears attuned to heaven's music.

Oh, my dear, sweet Shar, how I want you to know how very deeply I love you. I cherish you. I want you to know this beyond a shadow of a doubt. You are my beloved, as well as God's. And, indeed, we are all one. Your cheerful, faith-filled face and heart are a blessing to all of us here on this side of the veil as well. Please know that I can communicate with the angels of your loved ones. It is not necessary to know their angels' names. We all work together on your behalf and on behalf of your loved ones. We long to be of service.

My heart wants to continue to tell you how much I love you. But I'm going to close for now. I am so looking forward to being in touch with you. I long to kiss your brow.

With deep love and devotion,

Marianna

July 5, 2004

Dear Mariah,

Hello. My name is Michael, and I am your angel. My essence is loving-kindness. Because of who you are, my essence is very fully expressed through you.

I am so very happy that you and I are having this encounter. Donna does indeed have a gift from God, as Neal said at the Dream Work circle last Thursday evening. The support you gave her was a gift. The two of you have so very much in common, which is part of the reason you were drawn to each other at this time. You both love us angels. You both bring us so much joy. We want for both of you to be the joy that you are.

The work that you do is an expression of your deepest self. It expresses the loving-kindness that you are. May you be richly blessed for all that you do for others. We on this side of the veil see rays of light stretching way, way out from your being. You touch others in a way that you are quite unaware of most of the time. Let me assure you that you are very, very powerful.

Some do not see loving-kindness as being a powerful force in your world. Alas, some even see it as a weakness. Of course, those are the naysayers and they are to be ignored. Yes, my sweetheart, you are very powerful indeed. I am too, but that is not so important at the moment. What I wish for you to understand is the power for good that you are. Continue to do the work that you are doing, with full confidence that so, so much good is being done to bless those whose lives you touch directly and to bless your sometimes spiritually poor world.

Mariah, you are, indeed, my sweetheart. I love to watch you as you go about your day, as you choose the pillow with which you will sleep, and as you give attention to your beloved cat. I love everything about you. This is what I wish to express to you most of all—my love for you. You are so very beautiful; yes, so very lovely. Your sweetness brings me such delight that I can scarce take it in. Such sweetness. Such beauty. Such a soft and gentle heart—a heart full of love and caring.

Please know that I am **always** with you. You do not have to call me. I am already by your side. I know you have sensed my presence. What you do not know fully is my grand ability to help you in **all** that you do: Every message that you write for another. Every soul portrait you draw. Every reaching out you do to be of assistance. Ask me to help, so that I will be free to act quickly, ever so quickly, on your behalf. I want nothing more than to be your "right-hand man," to borrow a very human expression.

My sweetheart, oh, my sweetheart. Again, I say to you that I love you. Follow your dreams and follow your heart. May our hearts beat as one. Indeed, they already do; and this brings me so much joy. My deepest longing is simply that you know how much I cherish you. My heart overflows with love for you.

Michael, Your Beloved

July 7, 2004

My dear Beth,

How delighted I am that you requested a letter from me! You already know a little bit about me. My name is Annabelle, and I am your angel. I love you so very much, my dear! Yes, I am very dainty and fairy-like. You had a sense of me even before your mother passed on to you my description, given to her through Mary Ellen. At that time, many months ago, I was not used to talking. It has been my nature to be quite quiet. But, alas, we angels change and grow, also; and I knew the time would come when I would be talking with you. And here it is!

I am not so shy anymore. Let me tell you a little about myself. I live for the most part in the Elemental Kingdom, with my other fairy friends. We look after the plants and animals. I, myself, especially love all the animals. They are all my friends, and I am dismayed whenever I see one of them lost, afraid, or not being cared for properly. Pets are so dependent upon their owners. Animals in the wild are used to caring for themselves and do quite well, although the ever-changing environment is making this more and more difficult. However, it is animals left to the care of humans that often suffer the most. Too many are neglected and abused. Some do not receive the stroking and love they need to thrive emotionally. This makes me sad.

Each animal has his or her own angel or angels. Humans can pray for their pet's angel to care for him or her at any time, and especially in time of great need. I love animals so very much. This brings me to our relationship. You came into your present life with a great love for animals. This is why, at such a young age, you refused to eat meat anymore. This is why you get so very upset when you see someone hitting an animal. It is because of your very great love for animals.

What you do with this great love for animals is going to be up to you to decide. It simply is part of who you are and is something to be acknowledged. For now, my dear, you really have your hands full with that sweetest of sweetest babies, Aiden. He has become my delight, as are you. Each day I watch, as you love him, care for him, and enjoy him. Your mother has told you time and time again what a wonderful mother you are, **and you are!**

You have often been told that you are very fortunate to have so much help with Aiden, and this is true. But others are also twice blessed to have both you and Aiden in their lives. There is so much peace and joy in both of you and in the love that you share for one another. Why, just to see the two of you together lifts one's heart to a higher level. Do not underestimate your power to do good by simply being who you are.

We know that you are concerned about the next few years... getting your education, getting established as a family and all that. These are legitimate concerns. However, do not let these concerns rob you of the present moment. Babies and children are little for such a short period of time. Try to stay in the moment. Live one day at a time. Live one moment at a time. Savor the good of each day. Savor the joy and happiness of each stage of Aiden's growth.

You, dear Beth, have so much to offer the world. You are, indeed, an angel yourself. You appreciate all that others have done for you, and they know this because you express your appreciation so easily. Keep on expressing your gratitude, as you are and will continue to be in need of assistance; and it is so much easier for others to continue to help when they know that what they do for you and Aiden is not being taken for granted.

Your love for God is acknowledged. We want you to know this. God is very much with you in all that you do. Do not doubt this. God is love and you are one with God. There is no separation. Nor are you separate from anyone else. All the world is one. Someday this great truth will be accepted and lived, and the world in which you and your sweet Aiden abide will be a very different place. This is a very exciting time in which to be living. It causes us to rejoice! You, my sweetheart, cause us to rejoice!

Please be in touch. Talk to me often. I'd love to do all kinds of little (or big) favors for you. So, please, oh, please, feel free to ask. I'll hop off my little swing and be at your side more quickly than your can say, "Jack Robinson." I'm up and away, and yet forever by your side.

Love and sweet daydreams,

Annabelle

Beth's response:

Dear Mom,

Thank you so much for the wonderful letters from Christopher and Annabelle. Your gift is truly amazing, and everyone with whom you share it is very lucky. It comforts me to know that I can always call on my angel and she will be right there for me. Since I have learned Aiden's angel's name, Christopher, I have called on him too many times to count. Feel free to write to me from my angel anytime! Love, Beth

July 15, 2004

Dear Rochelle,

Hi, sweetie! Let me introduce myself. My name is Lisa, and I am your angel of light. I choose to call myself that, an "angel of light," because light is my essence. I am so light, in fact, that, if you were to see me, you would see me, but you would also see **through** me. My angel friends do not find this very amazing, but I'm sure humans would.

I really like to laugh, and I find myself doing that quite often. It is just a very natural thing for me to do; and actually, it is something difficult for me **not** to do. Why, there is just so much cause to be happy and to rejoice. Love makes me so happy that I laugh. Children make me laugh. The blue sky and green grass make me laugh. Quite frankly, I'm always just smiling and laughing, and am quite content to do that. All this brings me to you, my dear.

Your smile is magnetic. It is just so beautiful that when others see it, their own hearts smile and laugh as well. You have a light, a glow about you, which is felt by others and makes them want to sing. In reality, your inner light is touching something deep within them that connects with the Divine that is in all of you. Your sweet friend, Mariah, senses your highest self, your lightness, more than most because of who she is and her tender sensitivity to matters of Spirit. But please rest assured that others feel your goodness and lightness as well.

There are some things about yourself that do not please you. Please know how very much I love you, how much God loves you, and how much Mariah loves you. We want nothing more than for you to see you inner beauty and to love yourself with the highest of loves. God loves all of His creations, and you are, indeed, one of His. See yourself in this light: a child of God, deserving of all the good things that God has created. Know that you are very worthy, very worthy, indeed. You are His beloved and you belong to Him.

Please know that I love you with the greatest of loves. I have always been with you and would love for you to acknowledge this special bond that we share. I **am** your own special angel. I am yours alone. My desire and purpose is to be of service to you. I want only to be your friend and to live ever so close to your heart. We have such joy to bring to your world. Your world needs beings of light and laughter and happiness. Allow me to help you grow into your highest potential. **You are a miracle!** Let us make miracles together, my sweetie, my dear. Say to yourself often: I am a being of light. This **is** the truth about you that longs to find expression. Perhaps you would be willing to set the intention to be the being of light that you are. You will find the universe rushing in to greet this intention. Oh, for joy! For joy!

My sweet Rochelle, I love you and am so very happy to be speaking with you. May God continue to bless your friendship with Mariah. May all your dreams and wishes come true. Please welcome me into your life.

Love and more love,

Your Angel of Light,

Lisa

July 20, 2004

Dear Bill,

Hello. I am your angel, Sir James. You have known my name for quite some time now. But I have waited to write to you for a special reason. I wanted Donna's book to be near publication, and I want you to know that she has written many, many letters for others. I simply wanted you to know that this process of her communicating with us angels is, in fact, really happening. I thought it would be more believable to you if I waited a while. I hope this is the case.

My essence, Bill, is tenacity. If someone is tenacious, that person has the ability to "hold together strongly." This word is not commonly used in this sense. But I would like to use it in this sense to talk about you. You have had to be "tough." Life has not been easy for you. Your seizures and your medications have at times held you back from being all that you wanted to be and wanted to do. Sometimes you have felt different from others. School was not easy for you, either. No, things have simply not been easy. Yet, you have "hung tough." You have been a survivor, and you will continue to survive.

One cannot know what another has gone through if s/he has not walked in that other person's shoes. In other words, no one can know what your life has been like, what struggles you've been through, what your disappointments have been. You have not complained a whole lot about the hand that you have been dealt and have made the best of things. You are to be commended for this.

Please know that I care very deeply for you. I see everything that you do. I see the love you share with your cats. They thrive on your attention. I see the way you always

Down-to-Earth Angels

make sure Donna goes through the door before you do, even if your hands are full. I am well aware of the appreciation you feel for what others do for you. You have a very good heart. The love you still hold for your parents blesses them. May God bless you, too, dear Bill.

Please know that I am always close. Please ask me to help you in any way that I can. I would love to be of service to you. Donna was tired today. She kept plugging along. So, too, you have kept plugging along all these years. May your steps and your heart become lighter. May we become as a team, working together and seeing things with fresh new eyes. Keep your chin up. Keep your eyes focused on all that is good in your life and in the lives of your loved ones. You **are** loved! I have dedicated myself to you. Please call upon me. Please do.

Your own special angel,

Sir James

July 26, 2004

My dear, sweet Tabitha,

Hello. You know this letter is coming, and I am so very happy to be communicating with you through your Aunt Donna. This is going to be so much fun for all of us. I love to have fun. Fun just makes me laugh and smile and think about all the things in life that are so very good. You like to have fun, too, and it does my heart good when I watch you enjoying yourself.

My essence is warmth of heart. You, my dear, have such a warm heart. Your friends, your family, and those entrusted to your care feel this warmth and are enriched by it. You welcome others the way a warm fire welcomes others to stand near, feel comfortable and comforted. You are very much like a welcoming hearth.

You and I have been working together for quite some time, Tabitha. I am going to call you Tabitha, but please know that I love your nickname "Tabby," also. Both names suit you very well. Yes, we have been close for so many, many years. You, my sweetheart, have been working so very hard these past years to get your education in order to do the work that you are meant to do. My, how you have hung in there, perhaps feeling a bit discouraged at times, but never, never giving up. You will be such a source of strength and encouragement to so many. You have **not** given up, and you will be telling your story time and time again, letting others know that things have not been easy for you either. You will encourage others to keep on keeping on.

What a daring combination—a warm heart coupled with a drive to keep yourself and others going, even when things get tough. Know that there is much good in store for you, Tabitha. So much good. You will be getting yourself established: in your career, in your home, and in your personal life. You are on the right path. I want you to know how very proud I am of you and how very much I love you. Yes, I love you so very much. You have the most special place in my heart. I would like so very much for us to become very good friends and for you to get to know me and for you to allow me to be of service to you. Together we can work miracles in the lives of others.

All others have their angels too. You can ask others' angels and me to communicate, and we can all work together as a team. It really can and does work this way in the angelic realm. Oh, my heart is just bursting with pride for you and all that you have accomplished and will be accomplishing. You have been truly pruned to do the work that you will be doing. Others will love to be with you, just as others love to be with you now. What a warm, sweet, welcoming, friendly heart you have, my dear. It is aglow with love and goodness.

The drumming you have shared with your friends has been good medicine for you. It has nourished your soul. Continue to be open to ways to nourish your being. You truly are a spiritual being in a physical body. The spirit needs to be fed. Ask and you will be guided.

My dear, sweet human, know that I am indeed your own special angel. I have been with you since before you were born and will continue to be with you until you pass into the heavenly realm. May our warm hearts beat as one as we go about loving this world and helping others to feel encouraged and empowered. You have so much to offer

Donna Allen

others; we have so much to offer others. Know of my great love for you and of my great power.

With a heart full of love and warmth,

Maureen

It feels only appropriate to thank my husband, Rich, to whom the following letter is written, for his love and support through all my growth, searching, and questioning. He has always expressed confidence in me and encouraged me to explore and reach out. I am so grateful for him.

August 2, 2004

Dear Richard,

Hello, my dear friend. This letter has been a long time coming, hasn't it? It is because of your infinite patience that I have waited so long. You knew that you would not be slighted.

First off, let me tell you that I love you very, very much. You are, indeed, a good person in the truest sense of the word. You think of others so very often, putting yourself in others' shoes, looking at situations from their eyes, and meeting others' needs to the very best of your ability. You do, indeed, "love others as you love yourself." I love you for who you are and for your inherent goodness.

Donna is so very blessed to have had you for a faithful husband all these years. She has always felt your love and your concern and has benefited from your support and guidance. You have always encouraged her and given her the "slack" she has needed to grow and become who she is today. I could say much more about the fine husband, as well as father, you have been. But we will move on to others matters.

Gallantry is not a word in common usage in your culture today. Yet, you, my sir, are indeed gallant in the truest sense of the word. Brave, noble, high-spirited, daring, attentive and polite to women; this is Webster's definition of gallant and a fine description of you. At least, it captures in a few words at least *some* of who you are. In a way, though, it shortchanges you. You are much more than that.

You are love in the truest sense of the word. You are so very, very good. Oh, how I love you, Richard. Yes, my essence is gallantry and I share that essence with you in a very meaningful and powerful way.

You have your own brand of "religion." It is a spirituality that is lived and expressed in very practical ways: giving a ride to a co-worker, baking cookies for neighbors and friends, lending a hand to cut down a tree, writing resumes for those who've just lost their jobs, and always, always looking for a way to let others know you care with kind and encouraging words. Others gravitate toward you because they sense this caring and warmth. They let you know they think you are wonderful, and you are.

Yes, Donna has been writing angel letters for some time now. You have gently encouraged and allowed her to do her work even though you weren't always sure about "this whole thing." We thank you for that gentle support and the non-interference. It has been the perfect balance that she has needed. We want you to know that we offer you our support, dear Richard. We, the whole angelic realm, join together to thank you and to let you know we are here for you in any way that you need.

I take leave of you now, but I am always, always close. Please turn to me **whenever** I can be of service. Very much like you, I love to be of service to others.

Sir Walter and the Angelic Realm

August 3, 2004

Our dear Ginny,

We are going to speak to you, our dear, in a collective voice. We **all** want to be part of this message, which has been a long time in coming. You have been in close contact with us, though, and neither you nor we felt any urgency. But sometimes the written word possesses a power all its own.

We needn't tell you that we love you so very much. You have been our joy, our delight. Indeed, our essence, our trio essence, is Joy! You, Ginny, are joy and generosity of spirit in the truest sense of the words. Your joy and your generosity manifest in a myriad of ways — to the benefit of all those around you.

Your family, co-workers, and friends find that their highest and best selves are brought forth by you. You have a very allowing spirit and accept others for who they are. You bring out the very best in others and take joy in their successes and expressions of themselves. You truly know what it means to be part of a team, and others want to be on your team because you value the team concept so much. You appreciate synergy and know the whole is greater than the sum of its parts. This appreciation, more than anything else, has taken you to your current level of success in your career.

My, how you have learned to live in the moment! The simple pleasures of life bring you such joy: a walk with your sweet Morgan, a giggle time with little Mackenzie, a glass of wine shared with your dear husband, shopping or talking time with your daughters, a sunset, the birds, a small fountain in your office. Every day you take time to stop and smell the roses, even though your life is so very full and busy. You have lots of energy and do not waste that energy on trivial thoughts and small grievances. You move on quickly to what is good and useful to yourself and others.

You value the dollar and have manifested material wealth. This you have very generously shared with your daughters and other family members. You and Steve have been most generous with others and welcome them into your home and hearts. You both express generosity of hospitality unmatched in most circles. We angels love to be present and feel the joy, love, enthusiasm, and acceptance felt by those who enter the radiant circle of your home. Talk about "Home Sweet Home"!

You continue to be guided and healed through spirit communication. You are in close touch with your parents, grandmother, and other relatives. They love when you talk with them and appreciate your forgiveness work and rewriting of the scripts. You are deeply loved and appreciated by those in your family who have gone before you and who are still close to you and marveling at your love and success.

We have shared nothing new with you here, dear Ginny. This we know. But we did want to be included in Donna's book. Your sister and you share a very special bond. You have learned a great deal from one another. You share a very deep love and close friendship. Yes, it is a very, very special relationship and will last for all eternity. Such closeness is not to be taken lightly.

We close this written message with joy in our hearts. We are blessed to be your angels. We know this. Please continue **always** to stay in touch, as we delight in hearing

Down-to-Earth Angels

your voice and your sweet thoughts that nourish and bless us. Oh, how we love you, dear Ginny!

Your trio of angels,

Betsy (Elizabeth)

Grace &

Jonathan

August 3, 2004

My dear Tony,

I come to you with a heart full of love. You are such a joy, and **I love you,** and I love being your angel. I guess I'm being a little bit pushy. Donna had someone else for whom she was going to write a letter, but that letter, I promise, will be done on time.

I intruded myself upon Donna's sleep last night. I am just so excited to be able to make this contact with you, my sweetheart. How I have longed to make myself known to you in a way that you would not mistake as coincidental. Oh, I almost forgot to introduce myself. My name is Graciela, and I am your guardian angel. Yes, I have always been with you—loving you and guiding you. Most of the time you were unaware of my presence. But I was **always** there!

I am quite tall and quite powerful. I have long blond hair and am very beautiful. I do not mean this in an "egotistical" sense. But, if you saw me, you would think that I am beautiful. I love to be around animals and plants and spend a great deal of time with them. This I can do and be with you at the same time, since you love them also.

I love to watch you work with your big, strong hands—whether you are giving massages or working in your yard. You have hands of love, my dear, hands of love. Take good care of your hands, for they are an extension of your tender heart of love, and they serve you and others in the plant and animal worlds (humans included) very well.

The very best way that we can get to know one another is for you to be more open to feeling my presence, especially when you are outdoors. You will be able to sense me, this I promise you. I will take delight in your recognition that I am ever so close. I truly long for this sense of closeness with you, my friend and dear one. Of course, I can also be of great service to you. I am very powerful and very wise, and I know when to call on the help of other angels. Simply say my name, ask what you will, and then allow for what you desire to be manifest. Start with simple requests, please, so that you will feel the joy of answered prayer and experience a quick response. Some things take a bit longer, of course, but "with God all things are possible."

Tony, I am just so excited to be talking with you, so very happy. I do have a lot of energy and tend to run from here to there. I love being an angel. I love life. There is just so much to learn, to enjoy and to marvel at, isn't there? You are the love of my life. Please know this. You are truly a blessing to me and to others. Please feel my presence. I love you. I love you. I love you.

Your beautiful angel,

Graciela

August 4, 2004

Dear Marion*,

I know that your heart is heavy, and I am happy to be writing to you to lighten your load. My name is Tina, and I am your guardian angel. I come to you at this time at your request, but it is something that I have wanted to do for a long time. My essence is helpfulness. My greatest joy is found in being helpful to you and others.

Please let me mention that I know you, also, take delight in being helpful to others and do this on a regular basis. You are so very unselfish with your time and energy, and others benefit from your generosity. You see your skills as talents that are to be shared with others. You are to be commended for giving of yourself with no thought of receiving anything in return.

Your dear son, David*, has an angel, too, of course. His name is Bartholomew, and he is very happy to be making this contact with you. He loves David very much, stands close to him all the time, and wants very much to be of help. Bartholomew and I both want you to know that there is great hope, great hope indeed. There is no real need for concern, but this you might find difficult to believe at this time.

We believe that we can be of most help at this time by reassuring you that we really do exist, we are close at hand, we understand both you and David, and we love you both very, very much. You can talk to us any time, night or day, with the assurance that you are being listened to by hearts wide open. God is alive and well. He (or She, if you will) loves you very much. We are not separate from God; neither are you nor David.

We are here to serve you; you simply need to ask. You can talk to us about **all** of your concerns. We do ask that you try not to **worry**. Worry sets up energy patterns that cause that which you do **not** want to occur to do so. Bring your **concerns** to us and ask for guidance, comfort, reassurance, or whatever. Then be attuned to heaven's gentle response; it comes in many different forms, but the response will be discernible to you. Heaven often speaks in subtle messages, so try to take some quiet moments to listen to its gentle whispers.

Things are not too simple or easy these days for most on planet Earth. There are forces at work of which most are unaware. Most humans are going through growing phases and periods of discomfort. This is most necessary for the time being. Both you and David need to do things for yourselves that make you happy and bring you joy and comfort. Most often it is the little things in life that matter most. But, please, oh please, keep your chin up, keep your thoughts centered on what is good in your lives, and know that life is meant to be fully lived and **enjoyed!**

I am going to be closing now. Again, know that Bartholomew and I are close at hand and love to be of service. Please ask for our help. We cannot impose ourselves upon you. You are such a beautiful person, and I love you so much. Please be in touch.

Tina

August 16, 2004

Dear Jane,

I am so very happy that you have wanted to know your angel's name. My name is Heather. It rhymes with "feather." I say that only to be funny, because I am sure you know how to pronounce my name. I am kind of like a feather duster by nature. I like to go about making things look fresh and new, nice and clean and tidy. Most of us angels have an essential essence, and mine happens to be *organization*. However, *organization* sounds, to me, a bit dry and lifeless; and believe you me, **that** I am not.

Do you know what a blessing you are to Henry? Rest assured you are. Putting things in order for him is just what he needed. You are also a self-starter. He needs these qualities in you and is grateful for them. What a team you are! Donna is very happy that you are there at the office helping things to go smoothly during this busy transition.

Do you know that I have always been your angel and will always **be** your angel? Do you know that I love being your angel? Well, I do. It gives me great delight to see the joy you take in making surroundings look well organized, well arranged and welcoming! People tend to feel more at home, relaxed, and comfortable in such surroundings, but not all have the talent of creating such environments. One must have the ability to pay attention to the here and now, to detail. One must have a sense of what "feels right" when placing this or that item here or there. You have this gift, my dear. Indeed you do!

Please know that nothing happens by chance. Your working with Henry at this time is not by chance. Your coming to know my name at this time is not by chance. Nothing is coincidental. Knowing this is true can often be very comforting. I wish very much to be a big and important part of your life. There is so very much that I can and **will** do for you if you will ask. Please, oh please, remember to **ask**! I will rush, rush, rush to your side. I like to be busy, so please do not worry about keeping me **too** busy. I am happiest when I have things to do!

Feel free to talk to Donna about us angels. We are longing to be in touch with our humans. I am ever so grateful that you were open to learning my name, and I am confident we will become fast friends. I close with joy in my heart. This contact is so important to me.

With love and gratitude,

Heather

August 18, 2004

Hi, Cindy,

My name is Maxwell, and I am your guardian angel. I am very happy that we will be talking today and that we will be getting to know each other. Actually, we know each other quite well, but you were just not aware of that.

I love you so very much, my dear. This I wish to say to you over and over again. I have always been by your side. You have sensed my presence and have had a great deal of interest in angels and things in "the unseen." It is now time for us to truly work together for your highest good and for the highest good of others.

My essence is kindness. I love to do kind things for others, as it lifts their spirits, helps them to feel loved, and puts them in touch with that part of themselves which is God. In the very valuable work *A Course in Miracles* it is stated: If you must choose between being right and being kind, always choose kind. Oh, if all would only take those words to heart and practice kindness, what a lovely world it would be! Lovely, indeed!

Cindy, you are a very kind person. At your deepest level you wish only kind things for others. Many have been blessed by your kind words and acts of thoughtfulness and kindness. I would ask that you be tremendously kind to yourself. Things have not always been easy for you. You grew up with a mother who was not kind, to herself or to you. This was just not within her capability. A separation, emotional and physical, was necessary so that you could breathe more freely and grow more fully. Feel no guilt about this. You were trying to survive. I commend you for taking this oh-so-important step.

Donna has been blessed to have had you for a friend and neighbor all these years. Much time passes between your talks, but you both know there is a special connection of your hearts. You have learned from each other, and there is love there as well. May the heavens continue to bless this connection. Donna and you are one. Indeed, All Are One. Separation is an illusion. Separation from God is an illusion. Separation from one another is an illusion. One that is being dispelled. Hurrah!

Please call upon me often, Cindy. I am **always** eager to listen, to guide, to protect, to be of help, to be a comfort, and to bring love and light to **any** situation. You will find that even something as simple as saying my name will bring comfort, peace, and resolution. Together we can work magic! Wouldn't that be fun? To work magic together. Let's do that, my dear. Let's make magic together! Let's make your life all that you want it to be!

I close with love in my heart and with words of kindness on my lips. You are so very sweet, and I have asked the Most High to bless you abundantly! (As humans do, we angels pray to the Most High!) Blessed be all that is holy! Blessed be kindness.

Maxwell

Cindy's response:

I'm not very good with words, but I can tell you what is in my heart. Donna has been and always will be my angel here on earth. Love always and forever, Cindy

September 1, 2004

Dear Christine,

Hi, my sweetheart! I am your guardian angel, Leslie. You have been waiting for this letter, and I have been waiting to write! Finally, we two shall meet. My essence is loveliness. And you, my dear, are a **very** lovely person!

There is a lightness about you that is typical of us angels. We are not weighed down by all the troubles on the earth. We **see** the problems and the troubles, but we can also see **beyond** them. You have been criticized for not being realistic, for seeing things through rose-colored glasses. Oh, but isn't that a beautiful way to live? Isn't it lovely to be able to see the good and beauty in situations instead of always asking, what if? Continue to live your life on a happy note, my dear. It is, indeed, a very, very lovely way to live.

You have felt a very close connection with the angelic realm all your life. Is this not so? It is because you are one of us. You chose to come to the earth plane so that you could be an angel upon this beautiful planet. Yes, your origin is of the angelic realm. You have felt this, known this, at a deep level for some time now. Please explore this further so that you might understand your mission a bit more fully.

You felt a connection to Donna at the prayer meeting because she also is of our realm. This is something she is just beginning to accept. Sometimes these things take time. Do not be afraid of your true nature, of your mission. In fact, do not be afraid of **anything**! Instead, rejoice and be glad! Say proudly, "I am an angel!" Embrace this truth about yourself, and be glad that at long last you understand your tears, your questions, your wonderings. Your mission will be revealed to you in due time. In the meanwhile, let this all sink in. Let your being know who you are.

My dear Christine, I want you to know that I love you so very much. I am always by your side and long more than anything else to be of service to you. We angels communicate with our charges in so many ways. We can smooth the way for what you desire to manifest. We can call upon other angels for additional help, and we do so all the time. We love to travel and work in groups. I can help heal, guide, as well as bring love and thus loveliness to **any** situation. We never, never tire. We are sparks of the Divine and are expressions of the great Love which is the Divine. We are **very** powerful and work on behalf of our humans with tremendous joy and diligence.

I hope this letter is all that you hoped it would be. I've been waiting patiently. Donna has been quite busy, and school has started again for her. But I was so very often on her mind, as were you, and I appreciate that so very much. Please call upon me and know of my great love for you and my deepest desire to serve you.

Your lovely guardian angel,

Leslie

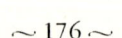

September 7, 2004

Dear Gina,

You have been very patient, my dear. Thank you for that fine quality of yours. My name is Belle, and I am your very own special guardian angel. My essence is beauty. My essence is very closely correlated to your highest potential, which is also beauty. And you, my dear, sweet Gina, are very beautiful.

There is inside you so much loveliness, so much goodness, so much beauty. This beauty shines forth from you in your smile, your sweet, gentle nature, your acceptance of others, and your kind words. Others love to be around you because of who you are and how you make them feel. You are a gift to so many.

You believe in the power of prayer. Please know that your prayers are like sweet whispers that rise up to heaven. Your loving, prayerful thoughts are energies that are swiftly snatched up by the powers that be and used to create that for which you are asking. Never underestimate the power of your loving thoughts and prayers. Prayers are creative. They bring into being that which is sought. And when groups come together to pray, such as at the prayer meetings held at Mary Ellen's office, hordes of angels are present. We listen and respond. We send out the alarm that this or that is being requested. Lo and behold, we get to work ever so quickly. Yes, prayers are heard and answered.

Gina, what is most important for you to know from this communication is my name and my essence, both of which have already been disclosed to you. My love for you is undying, and my longing to serve you, very sincere. I have always been with you and will always be with you. You create beauty for others by being who you are. Beauty lifts the heart, and all that lifts the heart is powerful. Thus, beauty is powerful. Continue to be the beautiful woman that you are. You enhance the beauty of the world.

You may talk to me any time, day or night. There is not one thought that you have of which I am not aware. Not one concern. Not one prayer. Not one longing. I hope that I am a comfort to you, a blessing to you. You are such a blessing to me. Your soft mention of my name will bring me joy. I will let you know that I am ever so close. I want you to feel my love, my power, my closeness, and my longing to serve you. You are so beautiful. So very beautiful.

Love and sweetest of blessings,

Belle

Gina's response:

Hi, Donna, I can't thank you enough for my angel letter. It brought such comfort to me. I sometimes wonder if I chose the right path in life. My angel letter confirmed for me that I did. It also reminded me that the power of prayer is real and that divine guidance is never ending. Hope to see you at the next prayer meeting. Much love, Gina

September 8, 2004

My dear, sweet Donna,

Thank you so much for being open to receiving a letter from me, your angel Samantha, through your Aunt Donna. Depending on your mood, you may call me Samantha or simply Sammy. I really have no preference.

You, my dear, are such a joy to my heart. I just love to be with you day in and day out, night in and night out. You are so busy and live such a happy, useful life that **my** life is busy and happy too. I do not have to worry too much about you. My main task is to simply nudge you here and there and then watch with loving thoughts and protective wings.

Thank you for going to Spain. That was a fun trip. I especially enjoyed Barcelona. More travel opportunities will present themselves in relationship to your work. **Please** take advantage of traveling when you are able. It is adventuresome for me, of course. But it also broadens your horizons, helps you learn what is going on in the world of healing in other locales, and helps you to appreciate the Oneness of All that Is.

Donna, you entered the healing world for a very special reason. You are a healer in the truest sense of the word. You bring love and comfort to others. You are open to the countless modalities of healing that are available. You truly want others to be whole and healthy. You are intelligent, have good study skills as well as an intense desire to learn. It is not by chance that you are working with a medical doctor who is willing to explore less traditional and conventional modes of healing. You will continue to learn much. Keep on keeping on with your nursing skills, your education, and your openness to all types of healing channels.

I would be remiss if I did not mention all the love that you share with your wonderful husband, Charles, and your beautiful daughters, Morgan and Mackenzie. With the help of your ever-so-loving parents, you have been able to "have it all"—a meaningful career, a fulfilling marriage, a gorgeous family and a very beautiful home. Yes, my dear, you have it all. And you know something—you **deserve** it all! May you continue to be blessed! Know that you are a blessing to so many others!

These words come to you from me through your Aunt Donna. She is very proud of you and to know you. You are open to her stories of love and healing and of Mary's comforting presence in her life, her words about essential oils, and her angel communications. You listen with an open heart and a discerning mind. You trust her sincerity, and you two are a blessing to each other and the world.

One last thing. My essence is that of healing. Healing takes place in so many, many different ways. Love is healing. Beauty is healing. Nature is healing. Touch is healing. Music is healing. Knowing that one is connected to All That Is is very healing. Dreams bring healing messages. This enumeration is by no means all-inclusive. Healing comes through the conventional/traditional medical community as well as the complementary/alternative health community. Obviously, thousands of books have been written on the subject of healing, and this process will continue. The goal of all of this searching is, of course, to help all life forms to become healed and whole, as the Divine intended. My essence is healing. This bears repeating. Your highest potential correlates to my essence, and this is why I asked to be your angel so long ago. We have valuable work to do. My job is to love, protect, guide, and comfort you and those you love and for whom you care. Never underestimate my power or the power of others' angels. We, also, are great healers. We are here to serve you. That is our primary purpose.

Donna, I just love you so very, very much. Please never doubt my existence or me. I am always with you. Always. Please talk to me, and invite me in to all the details of your life. Thank you for being open to my promptings and whisperings. You are just so wonderful!

With healing love and thoughts to you,

Samantha (Sammy)

September 8, 2004

Dear Stephanie,

Hello, my sweet child. Although you are no longer a child, but a fine young woman, I address you as such because of the love I have in my heart for you. My love for you is like that of a mother for her child. I hope this is all right with you.

My essence is simplicity. I like to keep things simple. When things are kept simple, it is much easier to enjoy the goodness of life. Clutter, too much stuff, too much busyness, and too much to do all contribute to a lack of peace and, well, a sense of unrest. You, Stephanie, also like to "keep it simple." Simplicity contributes to your sense of happiness and well-being. So, I encourage you to work to bring simplicity to your life in ever-increasing measure.

You have such a sweetness about you and an openness to the things of spirit. This is why this letter is coming to you at this time. Donna must stop writing letters soon in order that she might get on with the business of writing the rest of her book. But she cares about you very much and wants you to know that. I, of course, nudged her to write this letter, as I was anxious to talk to you and to tell you my name.

My name is Connie. I was instructed to choose a name when I found I would be in contact with you. We angels do not need names, but once we choose a name, we like very much to hear it spoken by our charges. You, my dear Stephanie, are my "charge." I have the privilege of loving and comforting you, of guiding you and of nudging you. It is my privilege to whisper words into your ear and to have you talk to me about all your concerns, your joys, and your desires. You may share your tears with me and know that I care very, very deeply. I can call upon the help of other angels for you or for those whom you love and care about.

You, my dear Stephanie, are deeply, ever so deeply, loved by me. Please call upon me. Say my name that I might help you in all areas of your life. Please keep it simple, as best you can, though life on planet Earth does seem to get quite complicated these days. Perhaps you can say, "Connie, help me to keep this day simple." I will show you little ways you can do that. Know I am always close.

With love and a love for simplicity in my heart,

Connie

December 27, 2004

Dear Kellie,

Hi, sweetheart. I am your guardian angel, Samuel, and I am so very happy to be talking with you. Yes, it is true that you have your own special angel. Do not doubt this. It will be my pleasure to be of service to you and to bring to you all the joy that you can handle.

Donna wonders, "What is his essence?" I tell you that my essence is "joy in doing." I am, indeed, a doer. I like to be busy, to be doing, to be on the go, to be of service. It is not like me to sit still for very long. I am always busy with the other angels, inquiring about their charges, trying to be helpful whenever I can.

You, too, my dear, like to be busy and on the go. You are a doer. This is something of which I hope you are very proud. My essence and your highest potential are closely related. So please continue on the path upon which you tread. Let us tread along together!

Do you know that I love to laugh? Yes, I love to laugh and to be busy. Perhaps some see me as being a little bit "scattered," but I assure you that this is not the case. It is just that I have lots of energy, and that energy needs to be expended. I have chosen to expend it in very helpful ways. In fact, the other angels know that this is my nature, and so never hesitate to come to me with their questions or to ask for help. They know that if I do not have the answer, I will research and find out information for them. I love to learn and to pass on what I have learned for the benefit of others.

My dear, sweet Kellie, you are learning so much, and I am very proud of you for this. Do not get discouraged about what you see in your field of study. Changes are taking place very quickly in the area of building good health. It is vital for humans to learn to take good care of their bodies, and new information will be coming forth all the time. One will have to run to keep up, but it will be worth the effort to keep pace. You have much to offer others through your own experience and through your studies.

Please know that I love you very, very much. You are my joy and my delight. I love to be with you, to work with you and to watch you go about your day with joy. Please trust me. Trust that I have the capacity to help you in all of your endeavors. You have a love for Michael. Know that he loves you, too. Do not hesitate to call upon him. I promise I will not be jealous. We angels turn to him as well. He is very kind and courageous and does not mind when we ask for his help.

I am going to close for now. But my heart is **always** open to you, always. Please talk to me; please ask me for assistance with anything that suits your fancy. Life is so very good, and you make my heart sing. Trust in all that is good. Trust in all that brings you pleasure and gives you joy. You are my beloved.

Samuel

Kellie's response:

I felt warm and fuzzy inside when I read my letter. It has so much love and guidance that I know it is something very special. Thank you, Donna!

December 29, 2004

My dear Mary Lou,

Hello. I am Theresa, your guardian angel who has come to you at this time after much longing to make direct contact with you. I was so delighted when you were included in Josephine's letter to Susan. Susan's heart was indeed touched when you held her precious little Leah and exclaimed, "Oh my, you can feel the love coming from this child." What sweet words to the heart of a mother from the heart of a mother such as you, who knows how to love so very deeply.

Perhaps this is what I wish to stress to you, my dear Mary Lou, more than anything—your expression of love is beyond that of most humans. You express your love in the most simple and yet most profound ways. And you do not tire of expressing this love day after day after day. We on this side of the veil commend you, applaud you and oh, how we love you!

I am with you day in and day out. I do my very best to give you courage and strength. But I must tell you the truth—it is you who gives me courage and strength. You give all of us courage and strength. Our jobs are not always easy ones. There are so many distractions on the earth, and many are not tuning their ears to the heavens and to us. We try to get through, but too often fail. So, perhaps you can understand how strengthened we are by those such as you who do love God, goodness, and the things of the ethereal world.

My essence is *longing*. This might seem like an unusual essence. And at this point in this communication I would like to tell you that your highest potential and my essence are closely related. So what is longing? Longing is an intense desire for something or for someone. Yes, intense desire. That is what longing is. So, what do I long for? I long to be of service to you. I long to lighten your load. I long to be loved by you. I long to be a part of your life as never before. I long for the heavens to open up and pour out blessing upon blessing upon you and all those whom you love and for whom you care. I long for you to treasure me in your heart the way I treasure you in mine.

I am finding words inadequate to express my love for you. Please talk to me as you would a trusted, beloved friend. Know that I will rush to bring to you whatever it is you ask. My heart longs to reach out and touch your brow and to offer you comfort, the same kind of comfort you give so readily to others. My heart longs to embrace you and hold you close. If there be tears, please allow me to wipe them ever so gently. Allow me to give to you the tender love that you give so very freely to others.

Mary Lou, you are so very, very precious. Others feel the loving energy that you exude. You are a radiating center of Divine Love. I ask the blessing of the Almighty upon you. Thank you; thank you for being my charge. You are my delight and my joy.

Theresa

December 30, 2004

Dear Barb,

I asked Donna to let me sponge ahead of a few other angels, as I was most anxious to talk to you. My name is Daniel, and I am your guardian angel. I have been with you since before you were born. We made a contract, and I have been honoring that contract all these years.

Let me tell you a little about myself. I am a self-starter. That is my essence; and as Donna told you this afternoon, my essence and your highest potential are closely related. Sometimes I might seem a little pushy, and I suppose I am. I just try my best to not hurt anyone in the process. I get a little bit impatient with those who hold back too much, with those who know what they want but just don't go after it. I have a difficult time understanding those kinds of angels and people.

You and Corky have taken on a very large task, and many, many are benefiting from your hard work. We thank you for creating this wonderful Wellness Center, this gathering place of healers and leaders and simply wonderful people who have so much to offer and to learn from one another. We angels are watching, watching ever so carefully, all that is going on in your special place.

This is why I was so anxious to get in touch with you. We angels are so very powerful, and there is much we can do to help. However, because you have a free will, it is imperative that you ask for our help. You can simply say, "Angels, angels, we need your help here." Or now that you know I am your own personal angel, you can say, "Daniel, I sure could use your help. Show me what to do." Any word or thought that gives me permission to jump in with my angelic powers will do the trick.

I know that you have lots of spiritual help, Barb. Please know this relationship—yours and mine—is very real. You simply did not consciously know about me. But—ta-da!—I am here, and I am real, and I want very, very much to be a part of your life and work. So, you might ask, "Where do we go from here?" I tell you, dear, sweet, Barb, the only way we can go is up! Up into a life of joy in service to others! Up in a life of peace and happiness! Oh, by the way, I love to drum too. Some think that angels don't like to drum, or don't picture us drumming, but as far as I'm concerned, drummin' is for everyone who wants to express him- or herself in that way. Yeah for drummin'!

I'm so delighted Donna followed her promptings to visit your Wellness Center, to buy her beautiful drum, to get to know her power animal, and to do a healing session for you. Gosh, I'm so happy you felt so peaceful after that time with her. Do take time for yourself. Your Wellness Center provides those times of healing for others. Don't short-change yourself in the process of providing for others!

I could go on and on. I'm just so thrilled I've had this chance to talk with you. Please talk to me, knowing that I hear every thought that comes my way. We are both self-starters, Barb. This is good. This is good. We know how to go after what we want and how to do this in a very positive, affirmative way. We will continue to bring much good to others. Please know that I love you very, very much. All for now.

Your angel,

Daniel

January 9, 2005

Dear Marilyn,

Hi, sweetheart! My name is Tiffany, and I am your guardian angel. I am happy you saw the angel "glowing" behind Donna at the neighbors' party. It caught your attention, and that is how I was able to touch your heart.

We angels have to use whatever means we can to get in touch with our humans. We can't always just "talk" to you, because too many think it is just their imaginations. Or if people do hear our whisperings, many think they are crazy and don't tell anyone and just shut out our voices. We've really talked to our charges for a long, long time. But people in your culture aren't used to this and so reject it as not being possible or normal. It really is quite normal, just not commonly accepted. Communicating with one's angel will be accepted in the not-too-distant future.

So, your daughter had a baby! We are so very happy for you and are rejoicing in this birth! We love when a new soul is brought into the world. Babies are just so sweet! Yes, they are a lot of work, and we do recognize this. This is why we are always available to help new parents and, of course, grandparents! Work! Work! Work! Tiring! Tiring! Tiring! But rest assured that we are close by and love to be of service.

Speaking of service, please know that more than anything else, I would love to be of service to you. My essence is gentleness, and my essence is closely related to your highest potential. So, it is appropriate that I come to you at this time, when you have the opportunity to express who you are—gentleness—in a new way, in the role of grandmother. What is more special than the role of a grandmother, who brings gentleness in so many ways? Marilyn, you do have the most gentle of touches, the most gentle of hearts, the most gentle of words. And you bless so many with your great gift of gentleness. You lift the hearts of others with your gentle, kind spirit and do not have harsh thoughts or words toward others.

We love to be of service and we love to be of support. This is why I am asking you to turn to me whenever you want someone to talk to, whenever you need a friend or a favor. Ask me to guide you, to show you the way. Talk to the angels of your loved ones. You do not need to know the names of the angels of your loved ones for you to communicate with them. Simply talk to them, trusting they are hearing you and responding to your thoughts and requests. Each and every one of your loved ones has an angel, whether they believe this or not!

Know that I love you very, very much. Know that I love your sweetness and your gentleness. Know that I am always near you, as close as your breath and your thoughts, and that I will always be with you. I am simply so delighted that I've had this chance to talk with you. Thank you! Thank you! Thank you for being open to receiving this letter. Thank you for being who you are.

All my love,

Tiffany

January 19, 2005

My dear Tamara,

It is my deepest pleasure to be writing to you, my love. I am so thrilled to be making this contact with you, as I have been longing to tell you of my love for you and of my longing to be of service. We angels each have our own personalities and desires and needs, very much like you humans. Many do not see us in this light, but I speak the truth.

My name is Joseph. I chose this name for a couple reasons. First of all, Joseph was the husband of Mary, mother of Jesus. He was loyal and faithful and fulfilled his mission so very well. We all owe a debt of gratitude to this wonderful man. He thanks me for the compliment. Also, well, I think the name Joseph just suits me. I am a man of strength and compassion; also, I feel my emotions very deeply, and my deep feelings do not frighten me at all. They are a part of who I am. I allow my feelings and take the time to understand what they are telling me. Too many men in your culture do not allow themselves to truly feel what they are feeling. But this will all be changing as men become more balanced and see themselves as both feminine and masculine. Women, too, are now more readily accepting their masculine sides. Both the feminine and the masculine in one's being must be embraced fully.

Your work is not easy. Indeed, at times it is very challenging, and you might wonder why you do what you do. Let me assure you that the work that you do is very valuable. You are touching the lives of many in ways that will live through all eternity. Not only do you touch those whom you serve, you touch the lives of those who work with you. You have a very loving heart and see quite clearly the needs of others. You reach out with words of love and encouragement. Do not think for one minute that your love goes unnoticed or that your words go unheard. No, all you do is having a far-reaching effect. As the pebble makes ripples in the pond, your goodness flows outward in an ever-widening circle to bless others. I commend you, my dear; I commend you.

I have been very patient. I have been on Donna's list of those who requested angel letters for some time. You, too, my dear, sweet Tamara are very patient. You are patient with life itself and trust that life is good and worthwhile and meaningful. You bring meaning to the word "lovely." You are lovely. You are good. You are devoted. You are kind. You are sweet. I see all of this in you and more. For surely you must know that I am with you day and night. I see your hard work. I see your joys and your struggles. I have been with you since before you were born and will **always** be with you.

I said at the beginning of this letter that I want to be of service to you. Please be sure to take the time to think of me, to talk to me, to bring me into your daily life. Ask me to help you with any difficulties you face, with any decisions you must make, with any tiny detail where an angel's touch just might "do the trick." I, like all the angels, am very powerful. Know that we wait, and wait, and wait to be asked for help. Unless it is a life-threatening situation and it is not your appointed time, I cannot act on your behalf without your request. So please remember to **ask**. I cannot emphasize the importance of asking enough. It is crucial.

I would like to leave you with one special word: *love.* Love is who you are. Love is what makes the world go round. Love is the power that can change the world. The love that radiates from your heart is powerful beyond human comprehension. So, please keep on loving as you do, my dear. You are a powerful source for good in your world. We angels love your world and our charges so very, very much. Please turn to me often.

With peace in my heart now that I have spoken to you,

Your angel, Joseph

Tamara's response:

Donna, your angel letter arrived in a timely fashion, just as angels do. Timely in the sense that the positive intentions and grace were a thing I needed—like the surprise of a cardinal in snow or a view of familiar stars after cloudy seasons. It was a welcomed gift. Yes, of course, you may include my letter. I'd be honored if Joseph's reaching out and sharing were something others would enjoy. Thanks so much for sharing your gift with me. Tamara

A couple days prior to writing the following letter, I did a healing session for Corky. He and his life partner, Barb (for whom I'd written an angel letter on December 30, 2004) co-own Inner Harmony Wellness Center in Strongsville, Ohio. I was quite surprised when I experienced little visions of cupids, pink and red hearts, and valentine "people" (the kind we used to cut out of colored construction paper in elementary school). Also, references kept being made to St. Valentine. Since Valentine's Day was almost a month away, I truly had no idea what all this information was about, and told Corky so. The following letter shed light on the subject for both Corky and me!

January 19, 2005

Hi, Corky,

My name is Cynthia, and I am your guardian angel. I hope you don't mind having a female angel. Sometimes people are taken by surprise if they have an angel with the sex opposite their own. But, I think you're okay with it.

The session you had with Donna kind of told you a little bit about me. I am very, very romantic. I love anything that has to do with romantic love, and so Valentine's Day is one of my favorite holidays. All those little red and pink hearts. All those little cupids that get neglected most of the year. All the joy and happiness of telling another "I love you." Yup, to me it is the very best day of the year. I just **had** to impose myself upon your healing session. It seemed like the perfect opportunity to pave the way for me to make my grand entrance into your life!

Actually, it wasn't a grand entrance. I entered into your life a very long time ago. Before you were born, actually. I wanted to have a charge who was handsome and strong, who loved life, and (would you believe?) someone who loved to drum. Why, drumming is one of my favorite pastimes. I have a very special drum, and I have owned it for a long time. It has flowers and butterflies on it. I love both flowers and butterflies with a passion.

Perhaps you can tell that I have a lot of enthusiasm for life. I know you do, too. Life is for living, isn't it? Too many walk around afraid to be who they are, afraid to express themselves. I am so happy that you express who you are, that you reach out to others, that you are open to the wonders of the universe and to that which is new to you. Please keep this openness. It will bring you much joy, and you will continue to touch many lives.

Life is so good when people are unafraid and when they refuse to be rigid. You allow others to be who they are and greet others with a warm handshake or hug that says, "Welcome." This welcoming attitude and heart is really what a valentine is all about, if you think about it. A valentine is sweet, light, happy, giving, and lovely—kind of like butterflies and flowers, don't you think?

Corky, my dear, sweet, Corky, you are such a prize. I am so very happy that you are my charge and that I am able to talk to you through this letter. To say you are a sweetheart would be shortchanging you. You are the bestest sweetheart! And so, I come to you, long before the official Valentine's Day is upon all of you upon the earth. But, I declare this day and every day a Valentine's Day for you, for you are full of love and goodness and sweetness and gentleness. And I want to express this love for you each and every single day of the year. Thank you for being open to receiving my love, my love!

Talking to you has been my true delight! Please know that I am always close. Always. You can talk to me whenever you wish. Trust that you are being heard. Trust that someone who loves you with all of her heart and who would do anything for you is hearing you. Please remember to ask for what it is you desire. We angels need you to ask; the asking frees us to act. (This necessity of your asking has to do with your free will and the way the Creator has designed things. We must honor this.)

I love your Wellness Center. It is truly a blessing to many. Please take time for yourself as you serve others. Attend to your own needs and continue to be open to receiving. This is very important. And so I close this letter with lots of love and lots of joy. You are my delight! Thank you for being my valentine.

Your loving and kind angel,

Cynthia

Author's note: Corky shared his angel letter with an intuitive artist friend, Tina, who then did an adorable drawing of Cynthia with her butterfly-and-flower-decorated drum. This redheaded angel insisted that her chin be resting on her drum, and that her dress be colored green. (Corky told me this made perfect sense to him, as he's often been called a "Green Man.") In the drawing, Cynthia is wearing a heart-shaped necklace and a sweet, somewhat mischievous smile. Both Corky and Tina sensed that this angel has a "bit of an attitude"!

Down-to-Earth Angels

Martha asked me if I'd be willing to type a second letter for her daughter, Lynne, as Lynne was going to be traveling to India and Martha wanted to offer extra support. (Her first letter is dated December 14, 2003.) I had never typed a second letter from anyone's angel before, but I immediately felt Huckleberry's desire to do this when she made the request. As I had done the first time I wrote a letter from Huckleberry to Lynne, I cried through typing most of the letter. I was very deeply touched by this angel's tremendous love for her.

January 25, 2005

My dearest Lynne,

A little over a year has passed since I communicated with you through the written form. The written form is not necessary, but it is something that is tangible and can be read again and again. My love for you has not changed; it is undying. It is unquenchable. I love you with a love that I do not know how to put into words. It is felt in the depth of my being. Know, my dearest, this love for you will not change.

So, we go to India again. The circumstances have changed, haven't they? You go to be of service. Do not doubt for one minute that all of the adventures you have experienced thus far in your life have helped prepare you for this trip. You will be blessed by your giving; your light and your presence will bless others.

The tsunami has been, in many ways, a terrible tragedy. This cannot and should not be denied. Yet there has been an outpouring of love and light such as your world has never seen. Those on this side of the veil are doing all that we can to alleviate the pain and suffering. We are helping those who are so afraid and lost; we are helping those who are helping.

Allowing you to go to India has not been easy for your parents. But you do now have their blessing. You go, my dear, with their love and their blessing. Not much more could be asked of parents. Yet, they are being strong and are willing to allow you to follow your heart's desire. They are to be commended. They will be blessed as well.

Lynne, again, please know that I go with you. I go with you knowing that you will be kept safe from harm's way, knowing that you will be provided for and cared for in the most generous of fashions. God loves you so very much. Yahweh is a loving God and sees the goodness and generosity in your heart. His love goes on and on, and so does yours, my dear, sweet Lynne.

I'm so sorry for the hurt in your heart. Oftentimes humans learn great empathy when they experience loss and sadness. But you are strong and courageous, and you will keep on keeping on. Know that I want to support you in any way that I can. Please, oh please, talk to me. Please, oh please, rely on me. Say my name often. Yes, I love adventure as you do, but what I love more than anything else is Love itself. Love is the flame that keeps the Universe in place. There is just so much power in Love. The power of Love must not be underestimated. It is Love that must be restored to the hearts of those who inhabit the earth. Love must not die. It is those like you who cause Love to be passed on and on.

This, my dear, is all I have to say at this time. I want to reiterate that I love you deeply and am with you every single moment. You are safe. You are blessed. And you are a blessing. Please stay close to my side.

Your angel,

Huckleberry

Lynne's response:

Down-to-Earth Angels

Hi Donna, Thanks so much for the letter from Huckleberry. It made me cry and cry. My life has completely changed in the last two weeks. I don't think I could change anything else if I tried. It has been so helpful to be reminded of the constant help and presence of my angel. He mentioned that the written form isn't necessary. I was wondering if you had any tips for how to communicate better? I feel like it's something I want so much but don't seem to make much progress. I often wonder what sort of being Huckleberry is—like is he even a he? It's a strange but wonderful feeling that someone loves you so much but you have no idea what he or she is like! Thanks again for doing this. It really helped a lot. Much love, Lynne

Author's note: Lynne's desire to know more about her angel, Huckleberry, prompted a conversation between Tina, the painter of my drum shown on the cover, and me. Knowing Tina to be a very intuitive person, I asked her if she would be open to receiving input from Huckleberry. A few days after my request, at an open healing session at Inner Harmony Wellness Center, Tina "saw" Huckleberry as a Native American angel with beautiful wings made of feathers from the bald eagle. She was built for distance and adventure, and was spirit-guided. Huckleberry was specific about the color of the huckleberries she held in her hand; they were red—the color of life and spirit! Huckleberry told Tina that she loves beads. She was wearing an amulet around her neck that looked like either a condor or an eagle. Her hair was dark black and long, with a few braids in it. Tina went on to say that Lynne's angel was very kind, and that she saw her doing things like canoeing in the rapids of a raging river and standing on the very edge of a cliff that overlooked the world. I passed all this information on to Lynne, who was delighted to learn more about her ever-so-loving angel.

Donna Allen

January 25, 2005

Dear Andrew,

Hi, there! My name is George, and I am your guardian angel. I hope you like the name George; it sounds kind of upbeat to me, which is why I chose it. I like things—songs, people, stories, and the like—that are upbeat. I know you do too.

So, there's really a lot that we could talk about. Life. Girls. School. Friends. Your auditions. But what I'd like to talk with you about for a moment is you and me. You see, I've been your angel for a long time now. All of your life. And I will be with you for the rest of your life. I hope that is a happy thought to you, because it certainly is a happy thought for me. There is no other person on the face of the earth whose angel I'd rather be. You were my number one choice. Yup, I got to choose you and, boy, did I make the **right** choice!

You might ask yourself why I say this. Well, I just love your enthusiasm, your joie de vivre. You put yourself wholeheartedly into whatever you are choosing to do. You don't do things because someone is telling you that you "should" do them. You follow your heart's desires and your dreams. By doing this, you are being true to yourself. This is good, my boy, very good.

Circumstances are such in your life that you are being given every opportunity to go after that which is important and dear to you. This is indeed a blessing. Not everyone has this chance. I know you will make the very best of the choices that come your way. I know that you will appreciate that which is given to you and that you will give back in overflowing measure.

Not a whole lot of men your age have the opportunity to know their angel first-hand in your culture. Not many young men would be open to this idea of his own personal angel. Yet, each and every one of you has an angel who loves you and wants to support and guide you in every way possible. We all love to be of service. Andrew, if you will say my name and simply talk to me, the joy that will be in my heart will be beyond measure. I am very powerful and can do so much to help you as you continue on your life's path. Please hold me in your heart and speak to me. I will hear every word you say to me and will respond in a way that you will understand.

You are my "charge," my very special charge. To be of service is why I am always by your side. Please know that I applaud you when you perform. I watch and feel proud. I will always be by your side to encourage, to support, and to applaud. Consider me one of your greatest fans. Do this, please.

With a heart full of love and support,

George

February 4, 2005

Dear Francesca,

Hi, sweetie! My name is Colette, and I am your guardian angel. Please let me tell you first of all a bit about myself. I come from a land very far away, from a galaxy far away. I asked to come to the area where you live so that I could be your angel. I wanted very much to be the angel of one such as you, who is sweet and kind and loving. There are many on the earth who do not know they are one with the Divine. It is hard work to be an angel to such a one, and I did not want that task.

You, my dear, know that you belong to God, the Creator. You feel a close kinship with Him and do not question His great love for you. You know that He is to be trusted and turned to in time of need. You know that God is neither He nor She. God is Being. But sometimes it is simpler to say "He" or "She." I simply have chosen to use the masculine form.

Joy is your trademark. Joy is your livelihood. Joy is the indwelling Spirit in you. That joy is what exudes from you as you live your sweet life and as you interact with others. And, my sweet Francesca, it is my joy to be a part of your life. It is my joy to be able to talk with you in this fashion. It is not chance that has brought about this connection. It is the work of the Divine, the lovely, lovely Divine, in your life

You are on the threshold of a whole new life, my dear—on the threshold of a whole new way of being and of looking at the world. Your eyes are opening to that which is good and true for you. Surely you must know how deserving you are of all the good things that God and the world have to offer you. Surely you must know how deeply you are loved and cared for by the Greatest Lover of all, God Himself. Please know that it is my deepest desire for you to know of the great love that I have for you, too, Francesca.

I could go on and on—about your sweetness, God's love for you, my love for you, and the divinity within you. But I'd like to take a moment to tell you of how I can be of service to you. You see, we angels love to serve those who have been entrusted to us. You have been entrusted to me, and I would love for you to know that I can help you in many different ways. I can whisper in the ears of those to whom you would like to send little messages. I can give you confidence and courage if you but ask. I can lead you to new friendships if that is what you would like. I can show you how to love yourself fully and to be open to many, many blessings. To be honest, there is very little that I cannot do. The trick, dear heart, is for you to ask. Yes, ask what you will and it will be given to you in overflowing measure.

Donna sees your sweetness and your goodness. She felt me nudging her to ask if you'd like a letter from your angel. I **knew** you'd say yes. And your "yes" made my heart glad! My angel friends laughed at my excitement. Perhaps it would be more correct to say that they shared in my joy and happiness.

So, sweet Francesca (I love your name) I leave this communication at this time. My heart is so happy, so very happy. Never before have I felt such happiness. My Francesca knows my name! My Francesca knows of my love for her! My Francesca and I are going to be building a relationship that will please us both so very much.

Donna Allen

Live your life, my Francesca, with all the joy and happiness that you dare to feel. Life is so good and you are so very good. At long last we meet. I sing! I sing! I sing with gladness! Alleluia!

Your loving angel,

Colette

February 4, 2005

Dear Cindy,

My heart is feeling a tenderness that longs to express itself to you in a way that you will feel and understand. This tenderness is deep and sincere and sweet all at the same time. It is a tenderness that penetrates to the depth of my soul. It...I'm at a loss for words. I just love you so very, very much, my Cindy. More than anything, I want you to feel the depth of this great love that I have for you.

Donna picked up immediately that I am the "serious type." This is true. To me, life is to be taken seriously. There is so much that needs to be done. There is so much love that needs to be shared. There is so much good that **can** happen. But I happen to believe that it takes work and dedication and commitment to bring all this about. So, yes, I do tend to be serious and I make no apologies for who I am. My heart is in the right place, my Cindy.

Let me tell you that my name is John. I chose this name as, to me, it has a very solid sound to it. It's a good, strong, solid name. I wanted such a name. I want you to know that you have an angel who is strong and solid and who is willing to work for what he believes in. What do I believe in? I believe that God is good and kind and loving, just like you. I believe that we angels can and do make a difference in the lives of those whom we serve. I believe that light is much, much stronger than darkness. I believe in the goodness of humanity and the universe.

So, you see, tenderness and strength go hand-in-hand. I am very tender, and yet I am very strong. I wish, my dear Cindy, to use my tenderness and my strength to enrich your life. Now that we have made this contact, you will be much more aware of my presence. Oh, I have been with you all along. But now you will feel my presence more strongly. You will know it is I who is whispering in your ear, supporting and guiding you. You can now call me by name, my sweet name. My heart will leap at the sound of your voice calling me. I will shudder with delight to be able to help you attain what you desire, achieve your goals, and have the deep peace that comes with knowing you are held and loved.

Know also that I love the sound of your laughter. I laugh with you when you laugh. Your laughter is music, sweet music, to my ears and my heart. I hold you in my heart every moment of every day and night. I watch you sleep and brush your hair from your eyes. I kiss your forehead and hold your hand. I breathe on you as God breathes upon all of Creation. You are my love, my everlasting love.

I love you. I love you. I love you. Trust in my love for you, my sweet Cindy.

Your devoted angel,

John

Cindy's response:

Thank you so much for allowing the spirit energies to flow through you in such a clear and concise way as to let me know that this angel was really speaking to *me*! After reading the letter a couple of times, I kept finding more subtleties inside his words by which "John" was letting me know that he really was around all the time. The sense of joy and comfort that comes over me while reading his words is really hard to express, almost like a vibration inside my bones that is calming and soothing—a sense of not being alone. I've always believed in angels and spirit guides, so I was surprised at how much an impact this letter had on me. I wish everyone could feel such a joyous connection to his or her angel. It has brought me such peace. Thank you, Donna, for providing an inspiring tool that helps me stay connected to a higher vibration and frequency of love. Blessings, Cindy

Donna Allen

February 4, 2005

Hi, Clar!

How unselfish it was of you to request a letter from Eric's angel before asking for one from your own. It's Donna's delight to be writing this for you and connecting us in this way. My name is Agnes, and I am your guardian angel. I have always been your angel and always will be. And it has been such a happy time for me.

You have such a sweet spirit and happy disposition. You have been "going through a lot," my dear, a lot—what with your feet and your concerns for your son and mother, not to mention your recent move. Yes, you've had a lot on your plate. Yet, you've remained cheerful and hopeful. You've maintained a grateful attitude, which has been admired by many. And it **is** admirable! To remain appreciative and faithful in the face of adversity is not an easy thing. You are running the good race, my dear, and quite successfully I might add!

So, you're in the healing business. Good for you! You are open to learning a new modality, and many are being blessed and will be blessed by your efforts! But please know that just being with you is healing for others. Your joy, laughter, love, and openness ripple out to others and "heal" them in ways that you do not see and of which you are unaware. Your energy, sweet Clar, is healing. To be in your presence is healing. Please be more aware of this, as this is true.

So, what would you like to talk about with me? Do you know that you can talk to me about anything and everything and that I am **always** willing to listen and to respond? I'd love so much for you to talk to me each and every day. From the moment you wake up in the morning until the moment you go to sleep. I'd love to be your number one confidante. That would thrill me to no end!

Phew! My heart leaps at the very thought of that. But perhaps that's too much to ask. How about this? Talk to me often, will you? Know that I hear everything—even that which is not directed to me. I "eavesdrop," if you will. I know about everything that is going on in your life.

Please see me as a very good friend. A friend cares very deeply about the other. And I care very deeply about you and all that concerns you. I am very powerful and am most willing to act on your behalf. Know that I can talk and work with the other angels. We are very interdependent and enjoy helping each other out. It's the way we work all the time. It's really quite fun!

I'm going to go now. My heart is happy. I can relax now that this letter is written. We will be in touch. Talk to me. Let me be of service. I love you so very much, and I love those whom you love as well.

Your sweet angel,

Agnes

Clar's response:

It was so special to get an angel letter from Agnes! I have felt the presence of protectors from the spiritual realm especially these last few years. To get a confirmation through Donna about this makes my heart glow with happiness. Now I feel my trio of guardians is complete—with Agnes being identified along with Michael and Regina, two of my angels whom I met a number of years ago.

Donna Allen

February 13, 2005

Dear Glenna,

Hello. My name is Hickory, and I am your guardian angel. I am so very happy to be in contact with you through this means. My name might seem a little unusual to you; I chose it because I love trees very much and prefer this name to Elm, Maple, and so on.

You, my dear, are in for a real treat. We are going to be having so much fun together. I do understand that you don't feel all that well all the time, and for that I am so very sorry. None of us angels like when our humans do not feel well, and we strive to alleviate suffering whenever we can. Please know that I care very deeply about how you feel physically.

Being outdoors is very good for you. Nature is a very healing aspect of your being. You can connect with the Divine through nature in a deep, spiritual way. Being with the trees, the air, the elements, and the open sky brings in healing energies and love from the universe. Be outside as much as you can, my dear. And know that I am with you always, whether you are inside or out.

Glenna, you are a very dear person. You are deeply loved by your family and friends. Know that God loves you very much as well. God's love can be a great source of comfort to you, and He wants all of his creations to know of His tremendous love. Never doubt this love. Treasure it as you would precious gold. Ah, it is worth much more than gold or diamonds or rubies. Know that God is love. Know that you are deeply loved by the Creator.

Donna has asked if I am male or female, as my name does not indicate which I am. Let me tell you that I am male. I am tall, with dark hair that I like to wear to my shoulders. Yes, I do have wings, and you might say, as you would in human terms, that I am quite muscular. I like to be busy with productive undertakings. While I do have a good sense of humor, I think, I do tend to be a thinker. Thinking is fun, I think. What do you think? That is just a little joke. Some say my sense of humor is "dry," whatever that means. Perhaps what some find amusing, I do not, and vice versa.

So, perhaps it is necessary that I tell you that I am very powerful. We angels all are. We like very much to be of help to our humans. And so, with a humble heart, I ask you, dear Glenna, to call upon me whenever you have a need or desire. Talk to me about all that concerns you, all that ails you, all of which you dream and for which you hope. I follow you every minute of every day, listening, observing and giving little nudges here and there. But it would truly be a blessing to me if you would talk directly to me. Please use my name when you do so. I spent quite a bit of time thinking about which name I would like, and Hickory pleases me exceedingly.

If I could wrap my arms around you and tell you I love you, I would. Perhaps you can visualize this. Please use your imagination to see me. Please converse with me. Please hold me in your heart and return your love to me. All of this would make me a very, very happy angel.

I thank you, my lady, for being open to this letter and to me, your angel. Thank you for allowing me into your life in this special way. We will be in touch. We will be in touch.

All my love,

Hickory

Glenna's response:

> Donna, Thank you so much for introducing me to Hickory. As Amy told you, I have been aware of his presence for some time. It is fabulous to be able to talk to him by name. You have given me a gift, and I cannot express the depth of my gratitude. Your letter has had a profound effect. Let me explain. Prior to receiving your letter, my pain was increasing to the point that I was spending most of the day in bed and was sure I could not manage much more without serious medication, which I have tried to avoid. I received your letter and thought how very kind it was of you to include me in your writings, but I was in so much pain that I just put the letter down. After a few days, I picked up your letter and read it over several times. I began talking to Hickory and asking him and God for their help. I told them that if I had to endure pain, I was willing to accept that, but I needed their help. I asked, prayed for direction, courage, and help in being kind to others. After a few days, I noticed my pain had lessened and my energy was increasing. My pain has continued to lessen, and for the past week I have actually had energy all day long. I have not felt this good in years. Talking about it brings me to tears because I never thought the pain would stop. I am so blessed to have Amy as a friend, and I am so grateful she cares enough about me to ask you for a letter on my behalf. The kindness the two of you have shown me is incredible. Thank you, Glenna

February 20, 2005

Dear Tina,

It is my deepest pleasure to come to you at this time. My name is Jerome, and I am your guardian angel. I know you have other spirit guides with whom you work. Please know I honor that, and that we all work together to bring to you your highest good.

Tina, let me tell you that I am very, very proud of you. You are using your gifts to bring not only beauty into the world but a greater understanding of some of the more mysterious as well. You are helping to bridge the gap between what are considered by many to be the realms of ordinary reality and non-ordinary reality. The veil between your world and ours is becoming thinner with each passing day. Your work is very valuable indeed, my dear.

You are growing by leaps and bounds. You are reaching new heights in your consciousness, and that growth is expressing itself through your work. Your consciousness is expanding. Donna experienced a sense of this expansion in your healing session with her yesterday. Be open to the flow of this higher consciousness. It is leading you to the place you need to be in order to do your work—your all-important work.

Know that you are very dear to my heart. Know that I love you very much. Know that I am with you as you work and as you play. Please know that I am here to be of service to you and that nothing would make me happier than for you to talk to me and to make your requests known to me. Life is meant to be enjoyed, and it is my desire that your work bring you all the joy that you so richly deserve. You are deserving of all the good that life has to offer.

Please be in touch, dear Tina.

Jerome

Tina's response:

Oh, Donna, you have me crying! This is incredible! When I first read the name, I thought, "Jerome? Jerome doesn't sound or feel familiar." Then I heard a voice say, "Remember the energy." And as I read the letter I kept seeing images of when I was a teenager. I remembered writing in my journal during all the hard times I had in my life. And there was a voice that would come through my journals named Jeremy who would joke, laugh, and encourage me. And then I asked myself what this had to do with Jeremy. Then the voice said, "Look at my name again, not as Jerome, but as Jer-o-me."

Then I thought…no, that can't be. That was something I made up in my mind to help me through my teen years. Now, as I read this letter, I am remembering the energy from the journal writing and I am feeling that same energy again. I now realize that I was channeling my angel all those times! Now I want to go back to those journals! That was a time in my life that my creativity was so open that I channeled without even realizing what I was doing! I feel like I've gained a piece of myself back! I am so very grateful for this. Thank you so much, Donna. This really means the world to me. Tina

February 21, 2005

Dear Dorothy,

Hi, my sweetheart! My name is Thomas, and I am your guardian angel. It is so much fun to be in touch with you this way. To know that I can actually speak to you in a way that you will understand—human words—is very exciting to me. For so long I've had to rely on heart communication, nudges and little whisperings in your ears. Now I can actually just speak what is on my mind. Wow! What freedom!

I would like you to know I truly like to talk and to play around with words. Words can be fun. Puns are fun. They make people laugh, and I like to laugh. Laughter makes my heart glad, and I know that laughter makes your heart glad as well. I love to listen to you when you talk. You speak with enthusiasm and have that little sparkle in your eyes that makes my heart sing. You are fun to be with, dear Dorothy, and have always been fun to have as my "charge."

Let me tell you a little bit about us angels. We stay very close to our humans. We watch and listen and offer guidance here and there. We talk with each other about what is going on in the lives of those we love so dearly. However, we are counseled to never interfere or to impose our own ideas. All human beings have a free will. It is a gift of the Creator. But—oh!—if we are asked for help, guidance, suggestions, or protection, we literally run to be of assistance.

That being said, sweet Dorothy, please turn to me often and say my name. Let me know that you would like me to be with you, to help you or to bring you comfort. My greatest joy is to be of service to you. For you to want me to be a bigger part of your life would bring me happiness that I could scarce contain. We angels love to discuss among ourselves the little details of our relationships with our humans. As a loving mother cares about the smallest details of her child's day, so, too, do I care about each and every minute of yours. I care about your wakeful hours and your sleeping hours. I care about what you eat and with whom you speak. I share all your joys and all your concerns. In short, I love you very, very deeply.

For someone who loves to laugh, I got a bit serious on you, didn't I? I just wanted you to know what was going on deep inside me so you would understand the depth of my love and concern for you. Once I know you understand **that**, we can have all the fun you want together.

My heart is light and happy! I have spoken with my Dorothy! You are my joy and my delight! I will rest easy now that we have made this most special contact.

I love your bubbly nature and your dancing eyes, my love. We will remain ever so close.

Your guardian angel,

Thomas

February 27, 2005

Dear Scott,

What a wonderful opportunity for us to be in touch! I am Bernard, and I am your guardian angel. I am very happy we have this occasion to talk, as you have been going through such a difficult time. Donna has already told you that we angels are always close and want to be of support to our humans. I am not always good with words and am going to rely on Donna a bit so I can convey to you want is in my heart.

You have been struggling a long time with many different issues. Personal issues. Family issues. School issues. I am well aware of all of these. I feel your heart being torn. You know what you want but oftentimes do not know how to manifest what it is you desire. Know first of all that you are very deserving of that which you long for. The longings of your heart are to be honored. It is important that you feel in the depth of your being that you deserve to be happy. Feeling deserving opens the door for one to receive that which is sought.

Know that the universe is kind and loving. The universe is very responsive to your thoughts and the feelings that accompany those thoughts. It is always wise to take the time to look at one's thoughts and examine what they are creating. What one thinks and feels is what one is creating in his or her life. Thoughts must be guarded. You want thoughts that bring to you what it is you desire. Thoughts of lack attract lack. Thoughts of abundance, joy, love and such attract all of that into your life.

Please know, Scott, that I love you very, very much. I am **always** with you. Please talk to me about all that concerns you, knowing that I am hearing everything you say. It is important that you ask me to help you, to guide you, and to show you the way. Know that I **can** do these things for you if you ask.

I hesitate to say this to you, as I do not want to distance you from me. But it is important that you be a little more open in your thinking. Sometimes you are a little rigid in your thinking. You think some things are just too good to be true. Please don't be upset that I brought this to your attention; I think it could be helpful information to you. And it is never my job or my intention to impose my will or my ideas upon you. Please just give this input a little bit of attention, would you?

The doorway has been opened for you and me. Our relationship is very, very important to me. Again, sometimes I am not very good with words, but I do know what is in my heart. My heart is full of love for you. I want us to be friends, very good friends. Please call me by my name. It appeals to me very much, and I'm happy I had a chance to choose a name.

Your angel and friend,

Bernard

February 27, 2005

Dear Alberta,

Yeah! I get to talk to you! I'm so very happy and excited that you asked Donna how you could know your angel's name! That one question opened the door for my entrance. My name is Alicia, and I am your guardian angel. This is just so terribly exciting that I get to talk to you and that we are going to get to know one another.

Actually, I know you very well, my dear. You have so much energy and so much enthusiasm for life. It is fun to be your angel. It's fun to watch you when you work, and fun to watch you when you are with your family. You just tend to kind of dive into whatever it is you are doing and go for the gusto!

Sometimes I have a hard time keeping up with you. I'm really just kidding because I like to be on the go a lot, too. There is always so much to do, isn't there? Some people sit around and are bored. Not you and me! No way! Being busy and helpful is the way we like to be!

I am happy you are so interested in the Indigo Children. They are a very special group of children who have much to teach. There are truly lots of special children being born at this time, many of whom have not been given any special name. Humankind is reaching new heights. This is, indeed, a very challenging time and yet a very wonderful time in which to be living. It is those such as you, who have open minds and loving hearts, who can help the special children adapt and develop as they should. Keep up the good work, my dearest!

I'm going to slow down just a bit in my talking. Sometimes when I get excited (which I am now that I am talking to you), I rush my words. But I'm going to take my time and tell you that my heart is full of love and appreciation for you, Alberta. I have always loved being your angel. You bring such delight to my life. You are trusting and good and loving. You have a ready smile and a heart that is willing to reach out to help others. You are kind and considerate. All these qualities and more make me grateful that I chose you to be my charge. I truly hope you are happy that I am your angel.

Know that I see and commend you for your efforts toward getting your advanced degree. This has taken a lot of hard work on your part. You are doing well to know how to approach delicate topics. Change takes time, and you respect this. Not everyone is as open to spiritual matters as you are. You take this difference into consideration in your work; it is wise of you to do this.

Well, my time is just about up for now. Know that you can talk to me any time and all the time. Please use my name when you talk to me. I just **love** having a name and chose it after much thought. I don't always put a lot of thought into something before I say it; but when it came to choosing my name, I thought long and hard before stating it. A name is a very special thing, don't you think?

Surely you must know how much I love you, Alberta. You are my delight and my joy. I love you as much as life itself, and **that's** an awful lot! Life is so-o-o very good! It truly is to be delighted in! So is this special relationship that you and I share!

Must run. We'll be talking. I hear everything you say and know your every thought and prayer. Nothing escapes my attention, dear one.

Sending love and hugs,

Alicia

Donna Allen

April 2, 2005

Dear Paula,

Hi! My name is Georgette, and I am your guardian angel. You have no idea how thrilled I am to be talking with you, my dear. This has been a long time in coming. You and Donna have been neighbors for all these years, and I've been waiting and waiting, hoping she would talk to you about her book. It is going to be a huge success, and many lives are going to be touched by her work. We angels are so very anxious to be in touch with our humans. This is very exciting for all of us.

You are such a hard worker, Paula. Please know that I recognize this trait in you and admire it very much. You are constantly giving to your family, with very little thought of anything in return. You give your time and energy, your love, your food, your very being—and do so very generously. Your children are blessed to have you for a mother, and your husband, to have you for a wife. Your sisters, as well, are blessed to have your love.

I listened intently as you talked with Donna over dinner last evening. You said you were jealous of those who have the "gift" of being able to communicate with those on the other side—be it departed loved ones, angels, or other spirit helpers. You also indicated that you might be a little afraid to allow these types of opportunities for yourself. Let me compliment you, Paula, on your candor. You really hit the nail on the head with your words, and you understand your feelings very well. Many are a bit afraid of what might be around the bend, afraid of the unknown, of that which cannot be fully seen or fully explained at this time. Let me assure you that your feelings are completely normal.

I might remind you, though, that **any** adventure involves a little risk. And delving into spiritual matters with which you are not familiar is no exception. This is where I can be of help to you. You could ask me to help you to not be afraid. You could ask me to lead you to those experiences that would be most beneficial to you at this time. You could, for example, say, "Georgette, I want to grow spiritually, but am not exactly sure how. Please guide me and help me to see and understand what would be most appropriate for me at this time." Be sure to ask, though, Paula, as we angels cannot act without your asking. Please talk to me as you would a familiar friend, for, indeed, I am a familiar friend. I have always been with you and will be with you until you are no longer on this earth.

Paula, it is most important to me that you know that I love you so very much. You are such a joy to my heart. I see your struggles, yes. But what I see most of all is your love. I listen to your words, yes. But what I hear most of all is your laughter. Your laughter is music, sweet music, to my ears and to the ears of your loved ones. Never cease to laugh. Your laughter is too precious.

Yes, the spirit world is becoming more and more accessible to humans, as the human race is rising up in vibration. It is important that one be aware of this shift that is taking place; it is part of the evolution that was intended for humankind. Many are feeling as if they are walking on shaky ground. This is normal when any major change takes place. Breathe deeply. Know you are safe. Know you are connected to the earth and to nature, and continue to enjoy that connection. You love the outdoors, and this is in your favor; continue to relish the moments you are in the fresh air and sunshine. They are so very nourishing to your sweet spirit and give you strength, hope and joy.

My dear, I am going to close for now. But I am not going to go anywhere. I am always by your side—loving you, guiding you, listening to you, and waiting to see how I can be of service to you. Please know that all of your loved ones have guardian angels too, and that you can speak to them even if you do not know their names. Not one of your words, prayers, or whispers goes unheard. We catch the prayer-thoughts of our humans within our angel wings, caress them with tender-loving care, and then speedily go about the business of bringing love and peace to all situations entrusted to our care.

Oh, my Paula, my dear, sweet Paula. Thank you so much for being who you are. I love you so very much.

Your guardian angel,

Georgette

April 2, 2005

Dear Vince,

So, how is my dear friend? My name is Anthony, and I am your guardian angel. Donna is reluctant to allow me to call you Vinny, but I don't think you will mind. It's good to be in touch with you, ole pal. This is indeed my pleasure, and I thank you for being open to receiving a letter from me.

I know this is all quite strange to you, Vince. Actually, there are a lot of things that are going on around you that probably seem strange and are different from what you were taught to believe. Some of those old beliefs are hard to shake. My only advice to you on this matter is to go at your own pace, keep those beliefs that are beneficial and helpful, and allow those that are no longer serving you to fall away. Changes are taking place on planet Earth at a very fast pace. Cling to what you know to be true and good. Be open, but don't worry about trying to "keep up." Listen to your heart and be who you are.

Perhaps it would be most helpful for me to explain how I can be of service to you. As your guardian angel, I am **always** with you. I know everything that has gone on in your life, as I have always **been** with you. Most of the time, you were not aware of my presence; but that does not mean that I wasn't there. My purpose in your life is to help you achieve that which you truly desire—in both very little and very big ways. In other words, there is nothing that you should consider "too small" for my attention, and there is nothing "so big" that I am unable to help you with it. Many people err on both of these counts, and I do not want you to do that.

You are very open in your sharing with others. I would truly love it if you would talk to me as you would a neighbor or friend with whom you are very comfortable. Just a casual chat would suit me fine. You are a very congenial person, Vince. You are trusting and good and know what feels right for you. You are genuine and kind and loving. I would go on, but too many compliments, I'm afraid, might turn you from me. That is the very **last** thing that I would want.

So, you know my name and you know that I'm your angel. What you do with this relationship is entirely your choice. You could put me on a shelf and there I would sit, unable to act on your behalf. **Or** (and I hope you choose this!) you can consciously take me with you wherever you go, include me in your conversations, and allow me to play a major role in your life. What would bring me more joy than I could express would be to be of service to you in any possible way that you could think of. No matter what you need—be it in simple matters on the physical plane or in more complex matters of the heart and in relationships—**I can** be of assistance to you. All you need to do is ask and allow yourself to be open to the different ways that I can communicate with you.

I go now, my friend. I go with a song in my heart and a hop in my step—full of joy that we have made this connection. You, dear Vince, bring me happiness. And may our relationship return to you the happiness and peace you so very richly deserve.

Your loving angel,

Anthony

Down-to-Earth Angels

A couple days prior to writing the following letter, I attended an "Angel Academy" presentation led by Kim Wasielewski, whom I met for the first time. Kim is a certified Angel Therapy Practitioner (trained by Doreen Virtue, Ph.D.), Reiki master and registered yoga teacher.

April 12, 2005

My dear Kim,

It is my pleasure to be writing to you, to be talking to you through Donna. What a special day it was for Donna last Sunday. She was so happy to be able to see you "in action"—talking about us angels and giving those present a better understanding of our availability to all. You are a good role model for her, and she appreciated your teaching style and humor.

You have known for some time that I am your angel. I, Abigail, love you so very much and am delighted that you enjoy so much being a communicator between our worlds. You do your job very well, my dear. You make those who come to you feel very comfortable. You listen very well to the messages that you are to relay, and you do so kindly, honestly and lovingly. You are very well suited for the work that you are doing on our behalf.

I want you to know, Kim, that our relationship gives me much joy. You trust me and turn to me so often. My heart sings when it feels you leaning toward me, and I love to hear your voice, your concerns, even your uncertainties. You are growing in trust—trust in your own self and your gifts and talents, as well as trust in our power and ability to be of great service to you. All of us, all of your angels and the archangels to whom you turn, rejoice when we feel you wanting our help. Please remember what you tell others all the time—you must ask! Then we can rush to your side to deliver whatever it is that you desire.

Thank you so much for being the kind and loving person that you are, Kim. You give so generously to your yoga students (both big and little), to your family members, to those coming to you for angel readings. Your heart is in the right place all the time. You want to be of service to others. This is very generous of you. You also know that God truly does want you to be happy. So many do not know this all-important truth. Yes, God wants all of His children to be happy, even joyful. Oh, how your world needs happiness and joy.

Continue on the path you have chosen, my dear Kim. It is a path of happiness and fulfillment through service to others. You are a blessing to so many and to your world. We are all here to serve you, as I've already said. And your serving others is helping to make your world a happier and healthier place in which to live.

My heart is your heart. I live so close to you that I feel your breath. I know your thoughts, your likes and dislikes. I know when you sleep (sometimes fitfully) and when you are busy moving about, which is often. Please know of my deep love for you, my desire to serve you, and the deep joy our relationship brings to me.

Your loving angel,

Abigail

Kim's response:

I am so misty right now after reading my angel letter. What a nice confirmation! I am very touched. I have to say that I have been doing so much angel "group work" lately that I have not focused in on Abigail. This letter has given me the opportunity to reconnect with her. Please be in touch and let me know how I can be of any help to you in your angel work. Thank you so much, Kim

April 18, 2005

Dear Alan,

Wow! How can I say thank you for being open to receiving a letter from me? Your talk with Donna prompted this communication. I was sitting, waiting, and hoping you'd be open to this idea, but I wasn't really sure. My name is Sir Raphael, and I am your guardian angel. Again, Alan, let me tell you that I am very happy and excited that you are allowing this to take place.

I have been with you this past year in a special way, my dear friend. Things have been very difficult for you, I know. One does not learn of such a health concern without going through all sorts of mental and emotional gymnastics. Hanging on to what you know to be true and good can be very challenging in such circumstances. Please know that I have been very close to you—offering any word of encouragement that I thought you might be open to. When you sank into depression, I was there doing my best to lift you up, to give you hope, to show you some light.

Alan, my heart goes out to you. You care so deeply for your girls. You care about your work. You have always been a very good provider and take your responsibilities very seriously. You have been carrying the weight of being a "family man" for many years now. Yes, there has been much joy—but there has also been the sense of burden, a burden that most fathers of four girls would feel. You have been doing your very best to provide all that the world has to offer to your family, and you have done a terrific job of that.

Please know that you have your own needs, too, needs quite apart from those of your family. You have the need to know who you are in the biggest sense of the word. You say that you are not a religious man. Yet, there is a part of you that is deeply spiritual. This part of you that is spiritual is in **all** humans. Yet, it is a part that many have been trying to ignore as they busy themselves with the "business" of daily life. A part of you has been searching for deeper meaning; however, the busyness of life has prevented you from taking the time to spend time alone.

I tell you all this only to help you be more aware of that which you already know. There is one Source. Many call this one Source by different names—and, yes, there are many different religions. I am not talking about religion, though. I am simply talking about a relationship, a loving relationship, with God—whatever your conception of God may be—and with your highest self, the self who is Alan deep within.

Oh, my Alan, my dear, dear Alan. I have seen your struggles. I have seen your caring, your friendships, and your love. You are such a good man, such a good man. I come to you at this time to tell you that I have always been your angel and have longed to make myself known to you. I want only what you want. In fact, what I want more than anything is for you to be truly happy and fulfilled. My purpose in your life is to help bring to you that which you truly desire. God—and again, however you think of God is perfectly all right—has given each and every human being a free will. No angel is permitted to interfere with the free will of his or her charge. That is why it is so important for you to **ask** me to help you in any way that you would like to receive help. I am here to be of service to you.

Please do not let the spiritual world frighten you. Just because something cannot be seen does not mean that it is not real. Love cannot be "seen" with the physical eyes, yet you of all people know how real love is. Most of the "things" in life that are truly of worth cannot be seen with the physical eyes. Some have the "gift" of being able to talk with and see us more easily than others. Some have been born with this gift; others have received special training. Just as you have grown from your own training and experiences in the area of law, so, too, others have spent considerable time and effort to hone their spiritual gifts. Oh, the world of spirit is vast and beautiful and something worth giving a bit of your attention.

Please be open to my very gentle presence and nudges. Trust your intuition and your inner knowing. You know that the drooping of your eye prompted the MRI, which led to the disclosure of your tumor. Yes, God's hand was in that. That was not coincidence. **Nothing** happens by chance. Nothing.

Alan, I love you so very much and always have. May this communication bring you comfort and a sense that All is Well. There is much turmoil in the outer world, and this will continue for some time. The place to find peace is deep within. Go within to find your peace and your joy. I am always with you. And I love you. And God loves you.

Your loving guardian angel,

Sir Raphael

(Additional letters will be included in the next generation of this book.)

Chapter Three

A Session with Neal: Be Your Joy

Drawing this book to a conclusion seemed to be an impossible task, as I continue to write angel letters and know that work will be ongoing. As I thought about some closing remarks, a session I had with Neal last month kept coming to mind.

Neal Szpatura is a shamanic practitioner, dream-work teacher, and transformational psychic. For the past year or so, I've attended his circles and classes at Mary Ellen Lucas' office and at the Ursuline Sophia Center on a weekly and oftentimes twice-weekly basis. The topics have varied greatly: shamanic journeying, dream work, intuitive and psychic development, dark-night-of-the-soul meditations, remarkable healing stories, summer solstice and winter solstice celebrations, teachings on Merlin, Celtic wisdom and faery healings—to name but a few.

Neal and I scheduled a one-on-one session for January 21, 2005, as I had questions I felt he could help me with. I had never had a channeled session with him before, although I'd heard he did this type of work. I explained to him that a couple of years prior, during a session with Mary Ellen, I was told I would be writing a book and that I had a main task or mission to complete in this lifetime.

The first question I asked was whether I could be given any more information on all of that at this time. Neal turned on the tape recorder, closed his eyes, and began to speak. A group of spiritual teachers from the other side of the veil spoke to me in a collective voice. The words "we" and "they" are used to represent this collective voice in the following transcription of this session.

* * *

"In terms of your overall mission—the essence of your mission and the hardest task you will undertake in this lifetime is to let yourself truly be happy. All human beings are born with a certain capacity to truly know the depth of connection with spirit, with nature, and with all that is. When *you* were born, you were born with an inherent capacity to have all of that, but to have it in a very light and joyful way. So the irony is that for you to be truly happy and to thereby complete your mission in this lifetime, you must do all of the spiritual exploring that you have been doing and will continue to do; you must continue to live your life; but you must allow yourself to explore moment by moment what it is that's necessary to do that in a joyful way.

"There are stories that come even from your Christian tradition of saints who are so full of light and joy, even in their earthly lifetimes, that everyone and everything around them becomes infected with that joy. There is an element of that possibility in your existence. That doesn't mean that you have to be ruthless in keeping a smile plastered on your face. But rather, you must be fully committed to understanding human joy, and how the interconnection between the realm of spirit and the realm of ordinary reality through the realms of nature and all that is, can foster that kind of moment-by-moment joyfulness—even through the most difficult of times."

They asked me, "Do you have any questions?"

After pondering a moment, I asked, "How far am I from that?"

"One of the important issues is to try to stop doing that kind of personal, self-judgmental questioning. It's not important that you know how far you are from it, but rather that you let yourself seek to explore what can be joyful in the moment, what can allow you to connect as fully as you find yourself capable of doing with spirit or with nature or with your fellow human beings in the moment, rather than worrying about whether or not you are doing it *right* or not.

"Letting go of being judgmental toward yourself is an important element in being as joyful as you can be. You're in many ways very accepting of others. You need to be as accepting of yourself. The exercise you explored in the meditation yesterday evening, allowing yourself to feel an intimate and deep connection with the Divine—that feeling, moment by moment, is the same as being joyful moment by moment. So, you tell me, how far are you from that? And don't answer that question, because that's not important. Can you appreciate that?"

"Yes," I replied. "But I think I need to listen to this again."

They responded, "You will be allowed to. Sometimes we do not show up on tape. This should not be one of those occasions."

At this point, Neal told me that they wanted him to check the microphone to make sure it was on. He said he hates when they do that. I found his grumbling quite humorous, and laughed.

They continued with a question. "Can you experience yourself—even in this moment—as the being of light that you are?"

"I believe so," I responded, after thinking a moment.

"That—letting yourself have that and taking yourself more and more to that place—is fulfilling your mission. And understanding that that is your pathway to fulfilling your mission is very important. Now, we will give you at this point that some of the *side effects* of your working toward your mission, or fulfilling your mission, will be several books, and a number of classes, and some very fine work as a spiritual healer. But those things are only possible insofar as you experience your joy. And tell the psychic that applies to him as well. We're getting bored with his depression!"

Neal took this last comment with a grain of salt. I couldn't help but laugh!

I asked Neal to thank whoever was speaking to me. "This is very freeing—very, very freeing."

"Good," they commented back, and went on, "Learn to love yourself in the moment, forgive yourself in the moment, seek your joy and be your joy in the moment, and know yourself as a being of light at all times. It's really very simple. Other questions?"

"My next question is—how can I tap into the wisdom of the universe?"

"You already do. What are you looking for?" they inquired.

"Something grander; something more obvious," I replied slowly, not even quite sure of my question.

"Be your joy. Know yourself as a light being, and be yourself as a light being. When you go to that place, you will then be in the wisdom of the universe. You will be in the presence of light. You will be the light itself. So, anything that you would call a technique that will enhance your capacity to be in that place, in that state, will help you be more consciously in contact with the wisdom of the universe. One of the most important things for you to do is to understand that there is never any division between you and the Divine. Any thought that that is the case is an artificial construct of the human race. And so, any technique, any joy, any experience that brings you into that place of being the light and being joy is also a state of being more fully in communion with and accessing the wisdom of the universe. Does that make sense to you?"

"Yes," I said. "And again, that's very comforting and very freeing. Sometimes I'm getting the impression or I have the feeling that I'm working too hard at 'progressing.'"

"Goddamn right!" was their surprising response, at which I once again laughed.

"So what do I do about it?" I asked in earnest. "How do I stop this drive? I've always been spiritually driven."

"Stop using that as an excuse, and let yourself simply be yourself. You have been given a slightly different understanding of what it means to be spiritual. And, yes, to be spiritual could mean to be on your knees eighteen hours a day for the rest of your natural life, but only if that is truly your joy. So, if you truly want to be spiritual, if you want to progress spiritually, be your joy. Be the being of light you already are. And, of course, there will be times when you will find things to read, things to study, things to explore, but let yourself do that out of joy, out of love, out of a way of bringing light into the universe. And you will then be spiritual. It isn't a matter of doing spiritual push-ups; it's a matter of being true to who and what you are.

"Try to work to tear down the sense that there is a division or anything that *must be done*. Simply let yourself be joy. Let yourself be light. Tear down the walls that separate you from true reality. Or simply let them fall away, because that's possible. There's no difference between you and Sai Baba, except that he has allowed walls to fall. Now, maybe he came in with some karma that made it more natural for that to happen. That doesn't mean that it is not possible for you. But don't take that on as an assignment. Don't make it something hard that has to be done. Own your joy. Be your joy. Be a being of light. You could never do a grander thing in your life than be so full of light that the entire world could be healed by it. It's one of those ironies, and one that you will give yourself some time to work with, I'm sure. More questions?"

"All that being said, are their any other healing modalities that perhaps I should learn, or should I continue with what I'm currently doing?"

They spoke to me with a slight tone of impatience, as if they were tired of having to repeat their main message. "*Any* that bring you joy. *All* that bring you joy. Understand that learning other healing techniques is not necessary to your ascension. Simply going after your joy—in whatever frame, whatever field, whatever moment-by-moment living—that is your tool and your path to ascension. We cannot give any more direct answer than that, because there is no more direct answer than that."

"Would you like to tell me anything at all about my angel letters and/or my book?"

"Definitely the right direction. Definitely going to be a thicker book than you think," they said.

"Can you expound upon that? Are you talking about more angel letters, or more of my own input, or both?" I asked.

"Both. Your book will go through several gestations. Don't feel that you need to be achieving a finished product immediately. You will come to understand that there will be a first and second generation, and possibly a third of that particular vehicle for teaching. Please don't let yourself be dismayed by that; let that be part of your joy. There will be more to be done through that specific vehicle. You don't have to hunt for something else."

My mind was racing and trying to take in what was just told to me. They asked me to please give them a response. I said, "I'm taken back a bit."

"Good. We like when that happens."

"So, are you telling me to be patient with the process and enjoy the process?" I asked.

"Yes, but, for example, because of what we're pulling from your turmoil that's going on…you could in a month or so consider your book finished, and you would be right. And you would be perfectly guided to shop it around, to begin to make it available for sale in a home-produced version. But then you will come to understand that there will be another version brought about by doing more work. So that there will be more material added from your perspective, and more angel letters that will be added. That's the way it is."

I told them that in some ways that information was freeing because I kept thinking the book was close to being finished.

"And you're right to do so," they replied. "But know that that is simply one doorway that will turn into another doorway. There will be another book that will, in fact, be another version of that book. Your joy will lead you to understand why and how. Some of it will be from some personal visionary experience."

"Will the visionary experience be part of this current book?" I asked.

"No."

I sat and thought for a few moments, grateful that I would have the tape to listen to at a later date, and time to process this new input.

"Please don't be saddened or distressed," they told me. "It's like having three children instead of one. They're all wonderful. And they'll be exactly what they're supposed to be when they grow up." A long pause followed. "Continue with your plans for the book as you understand them currently. Don't let this information redirect you in any way. But do see if you can find a way to get it produced so that you can think of selling it to the gift shop at Lily Dale by the opening of their season this year."

"What?" I exclaimed. "I don't understand that at all!"

"Listen to the tape," they said calmly and reassuringly.

Laughing out loud, I commented, "These guys are humorous! They tell me one thing; then they turn around and tell me another. But I'll listen to the tape, and I'll figure it out."

"Most likely," they responded.

Neal kept channeling (with a straight face, I might add), and I kept laughing.

"Now *that's* joy," they said.

I then directed a question to Neal. "Are you doing okay, Neal?"

They answered for him. "He's fine. We'll let him up for air if we need to."

I trusted their judgment and sat quietly—pondering for a few moments before I continued. "Okay, I think that's all of the questions I have. I don't want to pass up the opportunity, though; so let me think real quickly here." By now I was finding the whole experience very amusing, and couldn't contain my laughter. "This is all making me laugh. I've been taking everything so seriously."

In a half-serious, half-joking tone they said, "That'll teach you."

I chuckled in response. "Yeah, it sure *will* teach me. Marc's been telling me for over two years to lighten up!"

"Now you have a sense of how. Some of what's going on between us is a direct energetic transmission to help you have more of a sense of how that spirituality and that joyfulness can be one. And that's important. Your vibration will be slightly different after this work. And that's good. Simply embrace it, and know that it's part of the evolution that's appropriate for you in this lifetime. Listen to more of what you would call comedy, and let yourself be lifted up by your own laughter."

"I like Neal's jokes."

"He's grateful. We're not so sure." It felt to me as if they were enjoying having fun with Neal.

Continuing to laugh, I said, "We can stop any time, Neal. That's enough for me. Really."

Neal slowly opened his eyes, said something about getting back into his body, and called them smart alecks. It was obvious he was used to this humor from the other side.

"Are you all right, Neal?" I asked, still laughing at witnessing him being picked on.

"I'm okay. So, did you get information that was helpful?"

"I think so," I responded, smiling from ear to ear. "It sure lightened the load! Obviously I shouldn't have worried so much about what information would come to me through this session."

"Probably not," he responded.

Neal then looked downward and to my right. "I'm getting little visions of things. They're showing me your book. I don't know what your vision of your book looks like. But there's a little child down here who's got a coloring book that's based on your book. And there's a book of letters that are in response to your book. And there are some poems that are generated by classes that are taught from your book. So, I don't know if you were looking at doing anything like that, but that's some of the kind of stuff that I'm seeing. And it may not literally be you doing this work. Perhaps there are other people in ordinary reality who will be co-creating this stuff with you."

*   *   *

Neal and I talked for a while longer. I was still a bit confused as to what form they were suggesting my book take—a home-produced version perhaps…or perhaps a self-published version. It seemed, however, that I was being told to do whatever felt right to me. The decisions were mine; they were only offering suggestions.

Neal then asked whether I'd ever considered doing angel readings for others, such as Louise Cook had done for me. I explained that although that type of work was something I knew I'd truly enjoy, I had not as yet been led in that direction. It seemed to me that I was to continue writing angel letters—at least for the time being.

I thanked Neal for our time together and carefully tucked the tape into my purse. I knew I'd been given much food for thought. It was very comforting to hear that writing angel letters was "definitely the right direction," as doing this work brings me joy. It was also reassuring to hear, as my angel, Marc, had told me through Louise over two years prior, that my divine mission in this lifetime is to allow myself to be truly happy. Happiness need not elude me, or any of us. And I felt immensely blessed to have an angel whose essence is "lightness of being"—an angel who, by his very nature, has the capacity and desire to help me be joy and the being of light that I am.

Closing Thoughts

I would like to once again state my purpose for sharing this portion of my spiritual journey with you, and for compiling these angel letters into book form: to be my joy, to be a light, and to bring joy and light to you, the reader. Our angels want so very much to express God's love, to guide and protect us, and to be beacons of light as we journey on our life paths. I have considered it an honor and a privilege to be a vehicle for these angelic messages, and I have been humbled by this task.

I know that my work with the angelic realm has just begun. There is so much more I want to learn about communicating with these magnificent manifestations of the Divine. Each day I call upon my angel, Marc, and other angels and archangels to assist me in my daily life. Each day I am a little more open to receiving help and guidance, and to living more joyously and harmoniously.

You, too, have angels nearby who, more than anything else, want to be of service to you. Perhaps after having read this book, you have become a bit more receptive to the idea that angels do, in fact, exist. Or perhaps you've always believed in angels, but didn't realize that direct communication with them was possible.

I hope these letters have helped to convince you that your angels long to be in close contact with you. I hope your heart has been touched by the angels' tender messages of peace, love, joy, and hope. Yes, the letters came through for specific individuals, but I believe we all have much to learn from the wisdom and guidance they offer, and about the wondrous, loving nature of angels.

Is heaven on earth possible? Is experiencing the peace and joy of heaven in our daily lives feasible? I believe the answer to both of these questions is

Down-to-Earth Angels

yes. These heavenly beings desire to help us create peace, love, and joy in our lives and on the earth. The veil between the angelic realm and our world is growing thinner with each passing day. Together, we *can* co-create heaven on earth!

To contact Donna Allen directly, write to:
PO Box 1631
Willoughby, Ohio 44096
or:
Angelletters117@sbcglobal.net

978-0-595-35575-4
0-595-35575-7

Printed in the United States
32159LVS00005B/103-312